The Spirit of the Trail

SPECIAL EDITION

The Spirit of the Trail

A Journey to Fulfillment Along the Continental Divide

Carrie Morgridge

WITH ROSS SELLERS

Published by MFF Publishing
4242 East Amherst Avenue
Denver, CO 80222

Cover design by Sheila Parr
Book design by Alex Head

Special Full-Color Edition ISBN 13: 978-1-7322083-2-2
Printed in the United States of America.

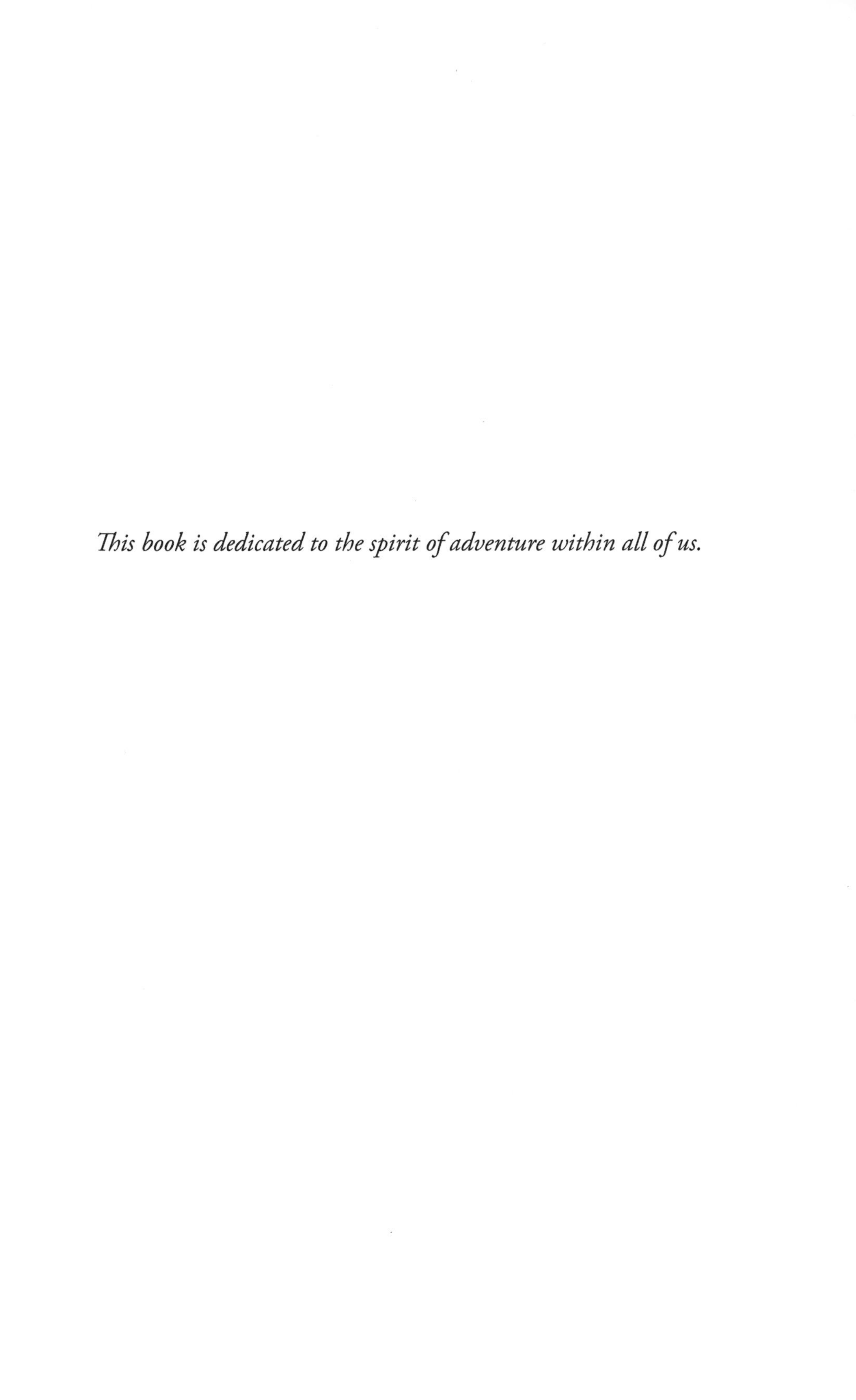

This book is dedicated to the spirit of adventure within all of us.

Foreword

You're going to do WHAT?! This was the first question we asked our son, John, and his wife, Carrie, when they announced that they were going to ride their bicycles along the Continental Divide from Banff in Alberta, Canada, to Antelope Wells, New Mexico, on the Mexican border during the summer of 2016. It is also the first question our children asked us when my husband, John, and I announced, at age 62, that we were planning to ride our bicycles from our home in California to our vacation home in New Hampshire during the summer of 1995.

John and Carrie rode their fully packed mountain bikes along forest roads and on single-track trails from north to south, crossing the Continental Divide 32 times. We, on the other hand, rode our lightly packed touring bikes along paved farm-to-market back roads and along semi-quiet highways from west to east over mountain ranges and through wide valleys. They often camped in remote areas, while we "camped" with Mastercard, staying in motels along the route.

The book you are going to read will tell you about John and Carrie's journey. This foreword will give you a glance into my husband's and my earlier bike adventure.

. . .

For both trips, research and planning came first. We read about others who had taken the ride and began our lists of what to pack, ordered our Adventure Cycling maps, researched what bikes were best for the trip, decoded how to get our bodies in shape, and perhaps most important of all—wondered what it would be like to be together 24 hours a day, 7 days a week.

It has been more than 20 years since our ride across the country, and rereading the log we wrote has been a lot of fun. We could imagine the places, hear the sounds, and inhale the smells one more time. Our goal had been to cross the United States, to experience the mountains, valleys, plains, hills, towns, and cities, to meet and talk with people along the way, and—of course—to enjoy the ride. Our route took us across parts of 13 states, from California north across Oregon and Idaho and into Montana, and then eastward until we reached the Great Lakes, where we dipped south before heading northeast to New Hampshire. Thus began our 4400-mile, 10-week "Amble Across America."

The kindness of people turned out to be a highlight of our trip. Two young friends rode with us the first day as we nervously cycled away from our home in California. Another friend met us on his bike at the top of a hill at the end of our first day and escorted us to his house for the night. Other friends housed and fed us along the way. We were saved from riding up many steep hills or fending for ourselves on busy roads thanks to advice from people we met along the way. In North Dakota the drivers waved to us, and across the country FedEx drivers were friendly and always gave us good directions.

The kindest person by far was John's brother, Dean. He thought we were crazy to ride our bikes across the country, so he offered to drive a sag wagon until the North Dakota border. In the American West, there are many miles between towns, food stops, and accommodations. In addition, we had cold, snow, and sleet. We could not have ridden there without Dean's help. He went ahead to find motels, he came to pick us up when we were finished riding for the day, and he drove us back the next day to start riding where we had stopped. What a kindness!

As two not-so-young bicyclists dressed in padded biking shorts, we were greeted with silence in small cafes as the locals glanced at us. Soon one brave soul would say, "So, where are you heading?" All ears would be tuned for the answer and soon we were having a conversation with everyone in the café. There is no better way to learn about places of interest, road conditions, and the best places to stay. We stopped at one café, located at a crossroads in the middle of wheat-growing country. Local ranchers had pooled their resources to buy the café so that they would have a place to gather. However, one thing surprised us, especially in the middle of the country. Many people do not stray far from home; information about a town only 30 miles away could be hard to find.

We learned how important wind and weather are to a biker. During one of our days in Oregon, we not only had high winds, but also cold temperatures and snow. Not great biking conditions, to say the least. We stopped at a rest area and found a place behind a sign where we could hide from the wind. A kind couple in an RV invited us in for coffee. They, too, were hiding out, waiting for the wind and weather to change. On days with a headwind we struggled to cover the miles, and on days with a tailwind we were able to do centuries—100 miles in a day.

Side winds, however, were the worst. A strong side wind can blow your bike over. Trucks are challenging for bikers under any circumstances, but on windy days they are especially challenging. Wind builds up behind a truck and when the truck passes, a blast of wind hits you—making it hard to keep the bike on the road.

Riding across the United States on a bicycle gave us an unusual opportunity to experience the vastness of the country: the varied topography, the beauty of the mountains and valleys, the isolation of small towns, and the density and tensions of the cities. Our gradual, one-pedal-stroke-at-a-time ride across the country also gave us a chance to experience the progression of the seasons—from spring in California, sprouting crops in the West, wheat harvest in the Plains, fresh sweet corn in the Midwest, to beginning of fall in the East.

Riding a bike also heightened all of our senses. There was the sensation of burning in our legs when climbing hills or mountain passes, and the delightful fear as we raced down the other side. While most days were pleasant, we had some snow and freezing temperatures, some rain, some lightning, and some extreme heat. We learned that different weather not only feels different, but also smells and sounds different. The best days were clear and bright when the birds were singing, the deer and the antelope were out and about, the forests and fields were in full color, and we were easily seen by cars and trucks. On bad-weather days cars and trucks do not anticipate seeing two foolish bikers on the road; we were easily distracted by slick roads and giant puddles. Not the best.

Perhaps our favorite sound was the singing of the meadowlark. Perched on fenceposts along the roads, the meadowlarks' enthusiastic, heads-back singing kept us pedaling. Quiet is not a sensation we often experience in our helter-skelter lives, but quiet is one of the luxuries of a bicycle ride along back roads and through the countryside. It allowed us to just experience the day and brought our attention to the small sounds of crickets and cicadas or the moo of a cow.

This country in so many ways is a real feast for the eyes. We saw pronghorn antelope in meadows, red-rock canyons gleaming in the sun, grasses moving in the wind, fields of grain as far as we could see, rushing streams that babbled as they rushed over rocks, forests, and mountains—off in the distance like paintings or close at hand where we could see their rocks, trees, and fauna. At one point a butterfly landed on the shoulder of my yellow biking shirt and rode along for at least five miles before taking off.

We stopped at historic sites and museums and saw firsthand how our country grew and settled. We saw a fawn that had just been born and was standing on its wobbly new legs. We saw families gathered for celebrations, and were even invited in for birthday cake. In both Minnesota and Wisconsin we rode on railroad rights-of-way that are now quiet, off-road bike trails, some with long, dark old rail tunnels. The trails pass well-tended farms and lead on through small towns that are former stops along the railroad. In the Lakes district of New York we stopped at a farm stand and bought the best peach I have ever tasted.

Every morning of the trip we were eager to get on our bikes, and every afternoon we were ready to get off our bikes. Toward the end of each day we would find an ice cream stand for our daily treat—a hot-fudge sundae for me and a root beer float for John. When you ride an average of 65 miles a day, you can eat ice cream every day.

Although John and I have been fortunate to travel to many parts of the world, our Amble Across America was an adventure that continues to give us great pleasure, stories to tell, and some of our fondest memories.

. . .

Now that you have read this foreword and after you read about Carrie and John's Continental Divide mountain bike ride, it is time for you to begin planning your own adventure. Do your research, get your bodies in shape, pick a ride, and just do it.

Someone is certain to say, "You're going to do WHAT?!"

—Tashia Morgridge

The Decision

The crazy idea started around the end of March 2016, when my husband asked me if I would consider taking an adventure trip with him. John had been digging on the web in search of trip ideas and was pretty sure he'd found us the perfect option. After several weeks of research, John landed on riding the Great Divide Mountain Bike Route, or GDMBR for short. The route travels through North America, so we would never be too far from our summer home in Clark, Colorado. To really pique my interest in this crazy journey, he informed me that the trail was actually a race, and that it was known as the hardest mountain bike race in North America.

Still, his pitch to me—his wife of 25 years—was going to have to be a big sell. I am very driven and I love my job at our nonprofit foundation. This trip would require me to take 60 days off work. However, I had been talking for a while about going to a "fat camp," as I called it, because of my recent back surgery—a fusion of lumbar 4 to lumbar 5—in November of 2015.

This surgery left me unable to work out for six long months and forced me to take a year away from my beloved tennis. My body had changed from pretty fit—I have completed one full Ironman and eight Half Ironman races—to pretty flabby. My regular workout routine was one to three hours a day, six days a week; but the surgery had made it hard to stay in shape, and I was in need of a serious jump start.

Hence the reason I was at least a little interested in John's trip idea.

I knew it would take something like this to totally disrupt my life. And, after several weeks of talking with John about the various trip ideas he was researching, I was getting pretty excited for whatever adventure he suggested. So when he told me that the GDMBR was the best option, I needed only one night to sleep on the decision. The next morning I said yes—I'm in.

We both considered how much this adventure would mean to us as a couple—from working together, to supporting each other, to having quality time and being unplugged. This was a time where we could work out, share the beauty of nature, and accomplish a grand adventure together. We were both all-in and ready for what it would take.

. . .

It's funny that sometimes you don't think about what exactly you're "in" for when you say you're "in." You know that you want to participate in the event, but you don't know exactly what that means.

Let me tell you what it means . . .

The Great Divide Mountain Bike Route is a journey from Banff, Canada, to Antelope Wells, New Mexico. It is North America's premier long-distance mountain bike route. While traveling across North America, you bike 2,774 miles on a route that is 88% dirt and 12% paved roads. You never stray more than 50 miles from the Continental Divide (also known as the "Great Divide," hence the route's name), and you have the distinct pleasure of crossing it 32 times—hitting the high point of the Divide on Indiana Pass in Colorado, at 11,910 feet. At the end of the trip, we will have climbed a total of roughly 180,000 vertical feet, the equivalent of climbing Mt. Everest *six times*, albeit on a bike and not in freezing weather or extremely thin altitude. Nonetheless, the "adventure" was not going to be easy.

Here is the total mileage of the route based on the state maps the route goes through:

- 257 miles in Canada
- 710 miles in Montana
- 72 miles in Idaho
- 489 miles in Wyoming

- 545 miles in Colorado
- 710 miles in New Mexico

The first major decision we had to make was incredibly important and would influence the entire trip. We could sign up for the Great Divide Mountain Bike Route with a touring group, go at their pace and enjoy the luxuries they provided; or we could go it alone, at our own pace but with fewer luxuries and more work on our end. As fun and easy as a touring group might be, we decided to travel the journey on our own. We knew this would be more challenging, but we also believed it would be more rewarding.

We called our family and friends to share the news of our journey and invited some of them to join us. Our Florida friends jumped at the chance. Barney and Krista Stotz would support us for a week in our pick-up truck from Montana to Colorado, making sure we had plenty of water when we crossed the desert lands of the Great Basin. Our longtime friend from Orlando, Mark, committed to riding the state of Colorado with us.

The Preparation

Once I was all-in, John went into overdrive with research. He started by reading books such as *Wilderness and Travel Medicine* by Eric Weiss and *Bear Attacks: Their Causes and Avoidance* by Stephen Herrero. John's biggest concern was our safety—from grizzly bear attacks to lack of water on the route. For as long as I can remember, John has been the one to worry. After years in charge of our family's safety, while our kids played in skate parks, went skiing or scuba diving, or tackled other adrenaline-inducing sports, John earned the affectionate title of Safety Sergeant. To this day, he continues to coach friends and family on how to be safe while enjoying various sports. However, he's also an extremely pragmatic guy, and he made research-driven purchases that would prove to be pivotal in our journey.

...

The first item he ordered from Amazon was a pair of high-performance socks. From that moment on, the packages just kept coming: shoes, more socks, Aquamira chlorine dioxide water-purification treatment drops, waterproof helmet covers, wool underwear, inflatable pillows, high-performance jackets and vests, earplugs, whistles, compasses, bicycle bells, tools and spare parts, cue clips to hold the turn-by-turn map pages on our handlebars, and so much more. Each day, Amazon would deliver things to our door—items John had spent hours researching.

Lists of tools and spare parts for an adventure like this could fill an entire book by themselves. Choosing our gear came down to a battle between weight and probability of need. Universal tools and "fix-its" like multi-tools, zip ties, and duct tape always seemed to work their way to the top of the list. (Even then, we would still find ourselves scanning the side of the road for a piece of wire, or even a rock or twig that might do the trick.)

The next big decision was which bike to purchase. The GDMBR has been done on more bikes than you can imagine: carbon-fiber race bikes with 20 speeds and old-school single-speeds; bikes with fat tires and bikes with skinny tires; tandems and baby carriers; state-of-the-art electric bikes and rusty old Schwinns. And even—unicycles.

Though the choices at first seemed overwhelming, we quickly ruled out unicycles and decided on the most reliable bike set-up: a steel frame, no shocks, tubeless tires, mechanical disc brakes, a Rohloff Hub, and—of course—a comfortable seat.

After researching the top mountain bike touring brands, we narrowed our selection to Surly bikes, a company based in Bloomington, Minnesota. Although they're a smaller brand, they have a loyal following and always get top-rated reviews. John found these bikes at Yawp Cyclery, a bike dealer near our office in Lakewood, Colorado; after a quick phone call, we were soon taking some test rides.

When John got to the model called "Surly Ogre"—yes, that is the actual name—he found the large frame fit him well, making it an easy decision for him. I tested a few bikes, but in the end, the large frame of the same bike (which wasn't actually surly at all) was the best fit for my body.

John's research concluded that we both needed to purchase a German-made Rohloff Hub, which is an enclosed gear-changing mechanism known for its dependability and smooth operation in adverse conditions. As usual, John made sure to spec out everything—from the Rohloff Hubs to the tubeless tires, handlebars, shifters, and everything else that makes a bike operate. The experts at Yawp confirmed he had ordered great parts, and they set to work assembling them.

The next big decision we had to make was whether we would use flat pedals or pedals that required us to "clip in"—attach our shoes to the pedals. As avid bikers, we were used to being clipped in. However, the blogs John read suggested that light hiking shoes on flat pedals would allow us greater flexibility in two areas: First, we would need only one pair of shoes for biking and walking after we reached our campsite. Second, by not clipping in, we could move our feet around on the pedals, and this extra movement and mobility would allow us to use different muscles while biking and give strained muscles a break.

Now it was on to deciding how we would carry our gear, food, and clothing. The options were either a lightweight trailer or panniers—packs that hung over the rear wheels. John knew that trailers received low reviews for the GDMBR, so we decided on panniers. They would fit on our bikes well and accommodate rough terrain.

After outfitting our bikes, we prepared in many other ways. We joined the Adventure Cycling Association and ordered all their maps and books, including Michael McCoy's classic, *Cycling the Great Divide.* Filled with important details on where to camp and what the journey would be like, this book would be our guide for the entire route. Next, we had to decide whether or not we would use paper maps the old-school way or track our progress electronically. We decided that paper maps would be more reliable paired with John's excellent sense of direction than a piece of technology that could break down at any moment and leave us in the dark—or at least staring at a blank screen.

We purchased maps specific to each US state and Canada from the Adventure Cycling Association. The distinct green-colored maps have elevation graphs that I became addicted to reading because I wanted to see where the hill climbs were and how hard each day would be. We relied on the maps to plan our food and water purchases and to locate hotels. Many times along the trail that was how we set our distance goals for the day—instead of camping, we would try to make the next hotel.

We coupled the maps with McCoy's book, and each night we would read suggestions on where to sleep, where to get food, and where to find water for the next day. We set a goal for every stop we made and had a fair idea of how long it would take us; John downloaded turn-by-turn directions and printed them on waterproof paper.

Now that we had most of our gear, it was time to start training. The McCoys, who authored that wonderful guide took 70 days to complete the route, and John convinced me we could beat their time. *Challenge accepted!* We knew we would have to train hard to reach our goal, but our competitiveness would prepare us for the task at hand.

In 2015, I wrote a book called *Every Gift Matters: How Your Passion Can Change the World.* In preparing for this trip, I decided I would blog about the adventure and see if it had legs for a possible second book. Since I have a website for my first book, I knew I could send my blogs and data to my office whenever I had an internet connection. John Farnam, my right-hand man, agreed to post my blogs on the website, and this allowed friends, family, and my readers to follow along on John's and my great GDMBR adventure.

The Training

John and I split our time between Florida and Colorado; we are Florida residents and really love living on the water. We take a lot of time appreciating the wildlife, the sea life, and the force and beauty of the nature that surrounds us. However, by June it's just too hot for us in Stuart, Florida, which is why we spend our summers in Colorado—truly the best of both worlds.

In June of 2016, we arrived in Denver, just as our specially ordered bikes were ready to be picked up. Yawp Cyclery fit our bikes to our bodies, and we decided to test them out. On June 14th we set off excitedly for our first training ride on the new bikes. Our excitement quickly fizzled when, just three miles from our home, John's gear shifter cable broke. His bike wouldn't change gears properly. With a broken bike, he sat on the side of the road, frustrated, while I biked home and grabbed our truck to get him.

He immediately called Yawp Cyclery, and they were incredibly supportive. Using FaceTime on the phone, John showed the technicians what wasn't working. They tried to support John over the phone, but we ultimately concluded that it was better to take John's brand-new bike down the valley and let the technicians at Orange Peel in Steamboat Springs make the repair. The technicians at Yawp Cyclery took care of it immediately—and they even paid for the repair.

On our training rides, we were trying to simulate what a day would be like once we were actually on the trail, so I practiced taking videos and pictures, tracking data on my CatEye cyclometer, and tracking our food and water consumption. We started our training rides without any panniers, but soon we were biking with them and adding more weight with each new training ride. The bikes alone weighed 37 pounds each, nearly twice as heavy as our usual mountain bikes; I needed time to adjust to that kind of weight.

Training for the GDMBR was different from the kind of biking we were used to. In the past, we had either road-biked to train for Ironman events, or we had taken our mountain bikes out on single track through various terrains. The type of biking for the GDMBR is a combination of both.

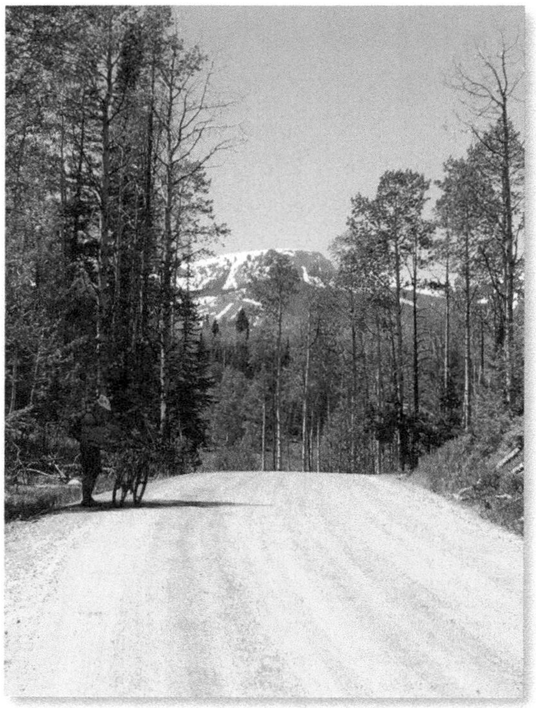

In addition, this was not going to be a race. Because stopping to take videos and photographs would be an important part of the journey, I realized it was something I needed to get comfortable with. While training we explored new roads, saw new sights, and discovered more wilderness in our own corner of Colorado. Training, it seemed, had many benefits.

When we weren't biking, we were practicing the logistical steps we would have to take daily in order to ensure that the journey went smoothly. We practiced pitching our tent in the house, so we knew how much time it took—realizing that if we were stuck in rain or a hailstorm, we'd need to pitch it fast so we could stay as dry as possible.

During this training period, I made our lunches each day so we could determine the amount of food we would need to pack for daily consumption. John and I had stopped eating red meat, chicken, pork, and dairy about five years earlier, so finding food that could sustain our energy and health on the route was a big concern for us. We measured how much water we consumed on each ride and tried to prepare accordingly. However, water is always the most difficult necessity to prepare for on long-distance bike rides, and there were more than a few times that water became a concern for us during our training rides.

We discovered that the GDMBR runs through Clark, Colorado, where we've lived for years. So we started cheering on the racers that came through, which allowed us to get a better idea of how taxing the ride could be.

The first racer to come through Clark was Mike Hall. We tried to catch a glimpse of him, but he was moving so fast that we missed him by 30 minutes! A few days after, the rest of the pack started to arrive one by one, and sometimes in pairs. John and I continued to follow all of the racers and estimate when they would be coming through so we could plan some of our training rides to coincide with just one short leg of their journey.

Pretty soon we were training daily with fully loaded bikes weighing around 65 to 75 pounds, depending on how much food and water we packed. We always stopped to talk with the GDMBR riders whom we were fortunate enough to encounter. One of the non-racing bikers we met on a training day was headed the opposite direction, riding up from Mexico to Canada. His name was Alex, and while talking with him we realized that we might cross paths with him when we started our journey in a few short weeks, in Canada; in other words, our first week on the route might be Alex's last.

Of course, we took the opportunity to ask Alex for advice and tips on how to manage the route. The theme that he kept mentioning was not to overpack. Most of the other "Divide Riders" we talked to said the same thing. Hauling any extra weight is a huge hardship on an already challenging route. While we chose to bike from Canada to Mexico, many of the riders we encountered were doing it, like Alex, in reverse—from Mexico to Canada. This allowed them to start a month earlier than we did, as Canada and Colorado can still have snow in June. Nonetheless, the Adventure Cycling Association had designed the route to be ridden from north to south.

. . .

Just a side note: In 2016 Mike Hall crushed the GDMBR record by finishing it in 13 days, 22 hours, and 51 minutes. This insane pace had him averaging around 200 miles a day—through snow, rough terrain, and 32 Continental Divide crossings.

By comparison, on Day 13 we had only made it to Butte, Montana, about one-quarter of the trip. It's no wonder that 60% of the racers in the GDMBR drop out.[1]

. . .

By the end of 21 days of training, we had ridden 667 hard-earned miles on our new Surly Ogres, and we were ready.

It was time for the journey.

1. Statistics courtesy of http://tourdivide.org/caveat.

The Travel

Travel Day #1
July 15

Can we really bike across the country and not get eaten by bears?

Our lives immediately begin to transform. Biking across the country and spending 60 days in nature on a mountain bike, while totally unplugged, is no small commitment. We both know that this journey will be life changing. That is why so many of the people we talked to before we left told us that completing the GDMBR was their personal dream, too.

Now our dream will become our reality. Just four months from when we made the decision, we are on our way to Canada.

...

During the week leading up to our departure day I had one last business trip. I was learning how to scale an idea. Much of the workshop was about how to achieve big goals by setting small achievable goals along the way. I didn't know it then, but learning that mindset would be very important to how John and I progressed through our journey.

...

We both wake up anxious. What if our bikes don't make it? What if we forget something? Will our bodies allow us to finish the ride?

John packs up the truck, while I finish up last-minute paperwork—this will be the first time since I was very young that I won't be working on a regular schedule. I am ecstatic. Of course there's a part of me that wants to check in on work, but I am ready to be unplugged, explore new territory, and not have to worry about work.

On the flight to Canada, John and I talk about our hopes and dreams for the ride. He wants to finish, and hopes his body will allow him to bike the entire way. He tells me he prays that I won't get eaten by a bear—though for some reason he doesn't worry that he might. And he wants us to come home happy and in excellent physical shape.

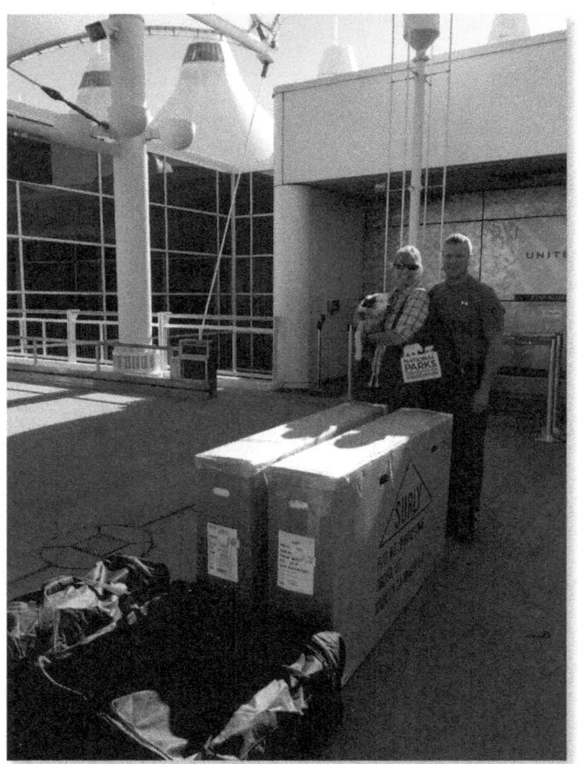

My personal goals are to rethink how I work, to learn how to take more time for myself, and to figure out how to make more time for the two of us. Though I set some big goals for myself, I intend to achieve them by taking the necessary small steps along the way.

What I am most looking forward to, though, is the unknown. I am not sure where the path will lead us. I'm unsure of the thoughts and feelings I will have, and I'm uncertain how this journey will change me.

But with eyes wide open, I am ready!

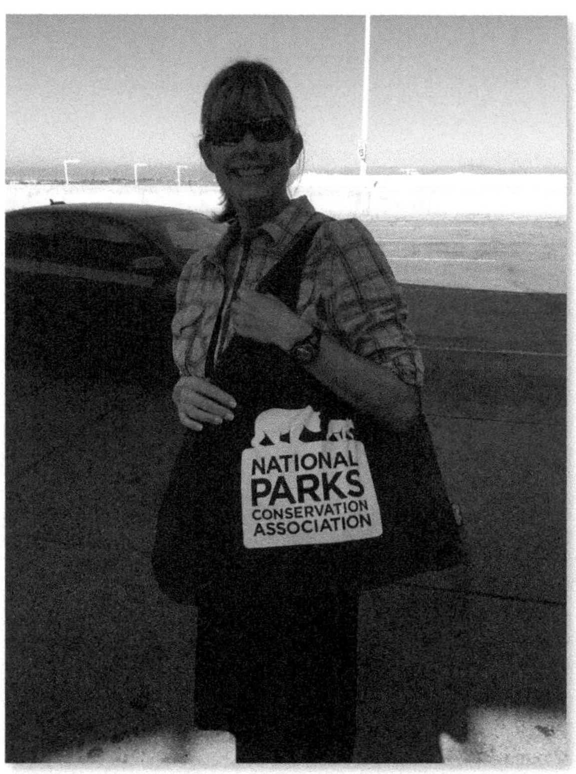

Travel Day #2
July 16

Our dream turns into reality.

Banff, Alberta, Canada

It's 50 degrees and raining the morning before we start our journey. Rain will become the norm during this first leg of the journey.

We enjoy a big breakfast and start checking things off our final checklist as we prepare to depart the next day. John assembles our bikes in the basement of the hotel while I plan our food stops and put together a list of what we need to buy in order to make it through our first few nights. I add rain booties to our list as well, because Canada has received a ton of rain recently—and more is on the horizon. If I can't find booties, we are prepared to put our feet in plastic bags before stepping into our bike shoes.

Luckily, we are able to find rain booties and everything else we need, including bear spray. Yes, you heard that right. We buy two cans—one for each of us. Quite simply, we will not pack a firearm, so the bear spray will have to do. The research John did said that bear spray has been found to be more effective than a gun against a grizzly—which does sound hard to believe.

At last we are ready to go, so we decide to check out the town a bit and relax for one more day before starting the grueling journey of biking across North America. We were able to purchase tuna, bagels, canned soup, tortillas, tea, one jar of peanut butter and jelly, Crystal Light drink mix, aluminum foil, and matches. We had been warned about the food through our research, and we knew it wouldn't be like biking through France from vineyard to vineyard.

While stocking up on some final items we meet the first of many active GDMBR riders—a fellow from France who had left Anchorage, Alaska, several months earlier and had plans to continue all the way to Argentina.

Just when you think you are about to start an epic journey, you realize "epic" means different things to different people.

...

Banff is a sweet mountain town very similar to Colorado's mountain towns. And man, do they have good food. It's gourmet, delicious, and innovative. John and I have the idea of eating at the Fairmont Hotel, but when we get to the Fairmont to scope out the trailhead for the next day's departure—and also to grab some lunch—we notice a TON of buses in the parking lot. So we decide lunch in town with the locals is a better choice—and we're right!

We are served hot tomato soup with red peppers and a beet salad that is incredibly filling. Oh, and a pizza to go. That's right—we will be chowing down on pizza for lunch tomorrow while on the trail. For dinner, Yelp helps me find a restaurant within walking distance of our hotel—The Keg Steakhouse & Bar. John and I want to eat a hot and hearty gourmet meal for one last dinner before heading out on the trail—amazing tuna tartare and stuffed mushrooms with veggies. For dessert we enjoy their famous coffee-mocha ice cream cake with chocolate and caramel. It's grand to enjoy one last amazing dinner before hitting the trail, where our gourmet dinners will consist of canned goods and any other food that keeps.

After dinner, we take a casual walk back to our hotel in a post-rain sunset filled with beautiful hues of pink and orange and the sweet smell of rain on pines. We go to sleep happy and, of course, anxious for the next day. All the preparation is now behind us and we are truly ready for the next morning—the beginning of The Journey.

The Trail

Canada

GDMBR Day 1
July 17, Sunday

Weather—Rain, overcast, cold
Banff to Canyon Campground, Canada

John's Notes: Banff to Elkford is around 110 miles and it looks like a hard two-day push. Still, I think it makes the most sense for us to do it in two days, even though that will mean we have to double the McCoy's book goal for day one. Canyon Campground is 61miles from Banff. Pushing hard through moderate-looking elevation will put us in Elkford by the end of day two.

Rain or shine—we are doing this!

We wake up to the sound of pouring rain. By 7:00 a.m. the skies are clearing, and we can see some blue sky. A vibrant rainbow appears on the mountain just outside our hotel window. We enjoy our breakfast at the hotel before leaving, and we appreciate our last hot shower and working toilet. We know what we are about to give up, and we savor each moment—the things we take for granted in life are often the most simple.

If there is a test to see if we can make it, day one is it. When we finally find the trail behind the Fairmont Hotel—it takes us 20 minutes to find the damn trailhead—sheer adrenaline takes over. Thank God John has great directional intuition. This is our reality now, and I am flooded with a mix of emotions: the excitement of cycling my first rotation on the path, and then fear: a fear of bears, and fears associated with not finishing.

Then comes hope. I am hopeful in our abilities and am resolved to finish the GDMBR in one piece.

The path is soaked from the days of rain leading up to our departure. It's wide, smooth, and empty. For the first hour, John and I are the sole riders on the trail. The only thing either of us can think about is encountering a bear. There were bear warnings and bear-proof trashcans all over town before we left, so it inevitably becomes the dominant thought once we find ourselves in their territory. Throughout the day, John whistles, rings his bell (mine broke in shipping), and talks loudly—about the bears. All are proven strategies that work to keep bears at bay.

Banff is surrounded by cascading mountains that are sharp and snow capped. The bike trail smells like fresh-cut Christmas trees as a result of the 16 consecutive days of rain, and it is wet and damp with spongy moss covering most of the ground. There is water everywhere. We cross over, and through, several streams along our way.

I mentally try to remain "in the present moment" as much as possible. This allows me to take everything in—from the sights to the smells to the sounds. I find that we are climbing quite a bit and moving slowly; in fact, with all the stopping I am doing to take pictures, along with our slow climb uphill, by lunch we are only 16 miles toward our destination for the night. At this pace, it's going to be an incredibly long day—our first campsite is still 45 miles away.

We are on the trail for about two or three hours without seeing more than eight people on mountain bikes. We continue to talk loudly and ring bells; John even develops a little jingle: "Yah oh, coming through." The bear-safety books John read said never to say "bear," unless you actually see a bear—at which point you should scream, "Bear!" and make noise to scare the bear away from you.

We don't want to see a bear!

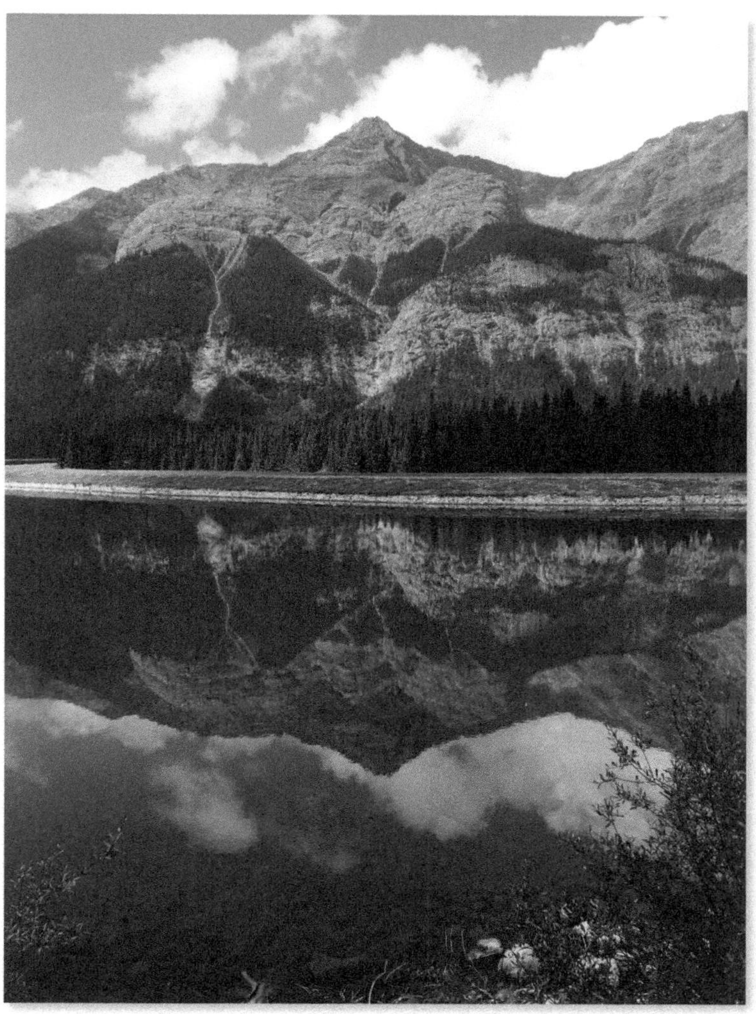

Once we get to Spray Lakes we enjoy 10 miles of flat pathway with an incredible view of the lake. It is visited by many bikers, fishermen, hikers, photographers, kayakers, and boaters. The trail by the river does not allow vehicles so we are able to bike side by side. John spots a bald eagle on the lake, which is crystal clear and should make easy hunting for the eagle. A large deer is lying down right on the bike trail; she doesn't bother to move as we pass by.

John is so excited to point her out to me that he turns his bike into the embankment and runs into a small natural wall, breaking his front pannier in the process. He is visibly displeased with himself—this is only day one, and he's already broken something? What else will break? Maybe the panniers were a bad idea, but they are all we have now. Anyway, it's a relatively easy repair—a couple of zip ties and we are back on track.

By the afternoon, we have passed all the people on the trail and are alone again. The maps and turn-by-turns have been spot on, but when you are in the wild and you come upon two trails, what do you do? Do you take the right turn as the turn-by-turn directions say, or do you take the hill because the map says? We take the hill, but discover that the turn-by-turn directions were actually the right choice. We quickly correct our route.

As the day progresses, the skies turn from sun to rain, and by 4:00 p.m. the sky opens up on us. It pours for over an hour, and even with our high-tech gear from REI and the new rain booties, we are soaked through—and cold. We calculate that we only have 16 more miles to our campground, but it feels so far away.

To our surprise, we bike upon a small lodge. Soaked to the bone, I enter the lodge to inquire about their room availability. They are SOLD OUT for the night. They have a roaring fire with comfy chairs and slippers waiting at the front door. The smell of dinner is all around, a dinner we will not be eating. Back into the pouring rain I go, and soon we are back on the trail, headed toward the campground.

We continue to climb out of the canyon, wet and cold. However, we're motivated because if we had gotten the room at the lodge, it would have felt like cheating somehow. Several miles later I get very hungry, so we stop on the side of the freeway and split a can of cold lentil soup and a tortilla. The next 16 miles are on an unpaved gravel freeway and downhill most of the way. When we arrive at the Canyon Campground, we are happy to find that there are tons of openings. We look at some sites and then find the camp manager. All of our food has to be placed in the bear box at night, so we pick a spot right next to the bear box—that way we can easily pack up in the morning.

On our first day it takes us a little more than 10 hours to make it to the campsite. I didn't know this at the time, but that will end up being a pretty average day for us throughout the trip.

The rain lets up, and we quickly pitch the tent. Because we've practiced pitching the tent in our home so many times, it's easy to set it up. We take our sleeping gear into the tent and find it's still completely dry. Next, I use the oversized bathroom to get out of my soaking wet clothes, and John makes a roaring fire with the campfire wood we purchased from the camp host. I cannot explain how great it feels to be dry, after being soaking wet for several hours. We use the small stove to heat up some tea and then eat some dinner—a can of tomato soup with rice. We lay our wet socks and biking gloves around the ring of the campfire pit. There is steam coming off them as they begin to dry, and I accidentally singe my socks. I only have two pairs of socks for the entire journey, so I need to be careful.

Our first official day is over. Though there are many more to come, I know that making it through the first day was a big test to see if we could really do this. I'm thinking that we can.

Ending day stats:

Start 9:00 a.m. Finish 7:15 p.m.
10 hours and 15 minutes
61 miles

GDMBR Day 2
July 18, Monday

Weather—Cold, sun, rain
Canyon Campground to Elkford, British Columbia, Canada

John's Notes: Even after a hard first day, the prospect of reaching the small town of Elkford is all the motivation we need because we know there is at least a chance we'll be able to find a room in a hotel, and enjoy a hot shower.

Sometimes you just get lucky.

I have been watching the weather in Canada on my cell phone app "My Radar," and for the first time in two weeks it isn't raining on the trail. We wake up rested and ready to go. It's still only 40 degrees, but we are anxious to start our second day. We find the beginning of the trail easy—this would, of course, change—but it's a nice way to start the day.

After a few miles on the trail, we stop at the Trading Post, the last stop for 50 miles with services. Shockingly, we bump into Alex, the same guy we met three weeks earlier on our training ride in Clark, Colorado—as he journeyed up from Mexico. Alex has been making record time, and was on the last day of his journey. We spend time talking about his journey and his plans for when he finishes. He tells us that he is used to zero comforts and that it will be hard to jump back into regular life. I share that Tashia, my mother-in-law, told me to take 30 days, after all is said and done, to re-enter what we consider "normal life." He concurs with her, and we part ways—he heads north toward his completion, and John and I keep trekking southward, in the midst of our day two.

By 12:30 p.m. we stop for lunch, and both of us are disappointed to see that we have only traveled 14 miles on a 56-mile day. We were also unaware that today would mark the first of our 32 Continental Divide crossings. But nothing can keep our spirits down. We are in the midst of stunning beauty, and there is not a soul around except for the two of us.

Hundreds, if not thousands, of butterflies have hatched on the trail, and we share the dirt path with them. Several butterflies land on my shoes and my clothes, as if someone from heaven is traveling along with us. I lost a dear friend right before we started our journey. I call her husband, Robert, to let him know that Bobbie is with me on the trail; in my heart, she is a beautiful butterfly and is showing me her spirit.

Our lunch spot is spectacular, with 360-degree views of the Canadian Rocky Mountains. During lunch, John notices that my pannier has lost a screw and is about to break. A quick repair with another zip tie and I am good to go. In the first two days we have already had issues with our panniers, and we're worried there will be more on our long journey ahead.

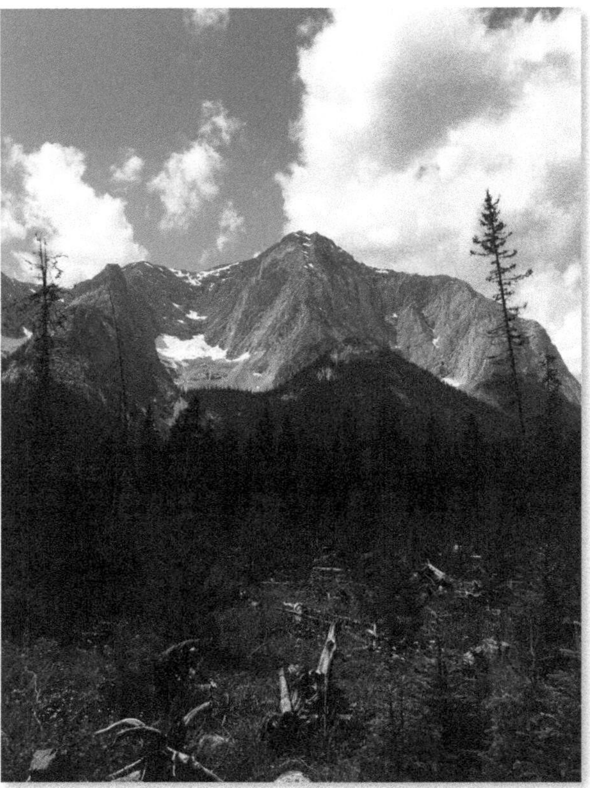

The afternoon part of the trail today is mainly on a dirt road, and it's a rather monotonous ride to our stopping point. At 5:00 p.m., just an hour shy of our destination, we witness a powerful lightning strike that's immediately followed by a crack of thunder that sounds like Indiana Jones's whip. Rain seems inevitable, but we luckily make it to our destination without getting soaked as we did yesterday.

The hotel in Elkford has a vacancy, and after a long day on the trail we are pleased to get a modest room. The hotel is GDMBR-rider friendly and has a hose for us to spray down our bikes before we wheel them into the room. Once we unpack our bikes it's time to enjoy a nice hot shower—*glorious.*

A local pizza parlor is near our hotel, and as we walk up we notice three geared-up mountain bikes outside the front door.

As we enter, we find the dining room to be an open-concept restaurant with tables for four. The three men whose bikes are outside end up being from Colorado, and the young single guy at another table is a recent college grad, Jake, from Kansas. We all talk about the trail and how hard it truly is, and each of us has aspirations to conquer the GDMBR. We hope that Jake will join us tomorrow, as he seems a little lonely on the trail by himself.

Ending day stats:

Start 9:15 a.m. Finish 6:15 p.m.
9 hours
56.8 miles

GDMBR Day 3
July 19, Tuesday

Weather—Sun
Elkford to Fernie, Canada

John's Notes: The previous night was filled with contemplation; would we take the newly established main route or the older alternate? The new route through the upper Flathead and Wigwam River Valley is 40 miles longer, has no services, and is one of the remotest grizzly bear–infested sections of the GDMBR. One of our primary objectives is to finish the GDMBR and not get eaten by a grizzly bear. The Fernie alternate makes sense for safety and comfort reasons. The idea of choosing the alternate so early in our journey, and missing the beauty of the main route, feels like the right decision—but a bit of a cop-out nonetheless.

When the road is washed out . . .
what path do you take?

For breakfast I have a can of tomato soup and homemade zucchini bread while John enjoys a homemade cinnamon bun and zucchini bread.

Between our hotel and the gas station, there is a mother deer casually lying in the grass, and she doesn't move as we pass by. When we bike back from the gas station, her two babies with spots on their backs join her. None of them seems to even care or notice that we are directly next to them, which is a pretty cool way to start the morning.

Our journey starts up the valley with a 2.4-mile hill climb that instantly warms our bodies. The views are incredible from the top. I have to laugh as we pass a sign pointing out "viewpoint". Eventually, we encounter the part of the trail that's washed out, which was the topic in the pizza parlor last night. It only takes John a few seconds to see an alternate route. We descend down the steep rocky hill and walk along the roaring river. It was a little unnerving to walk a bike that close to the Elk River—one wrong step and we would have been swept away.

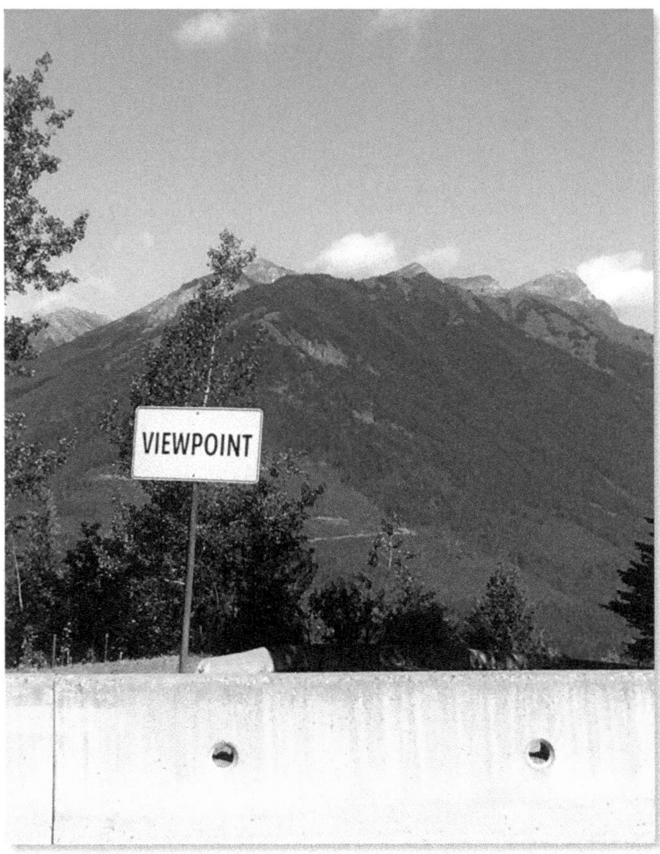

The terrain is so rocky and steep that John has to remove the panniers from both of our bikes and lug them up the hill before we can push our bikes up. Physically I don't have the strength to push my own bike up the steep hill, so John has to do it for me.

After our little diversion, the trail has us on paved roads the rest of the day. We spot a sign for an airport and stop for a snack while sharing a conversation with a local pilot. John is a pilot himself, and they talk about airplanes and local aviation. Unfortunately, right when we leave we are greeted by a headwind, and it doesn't stop.

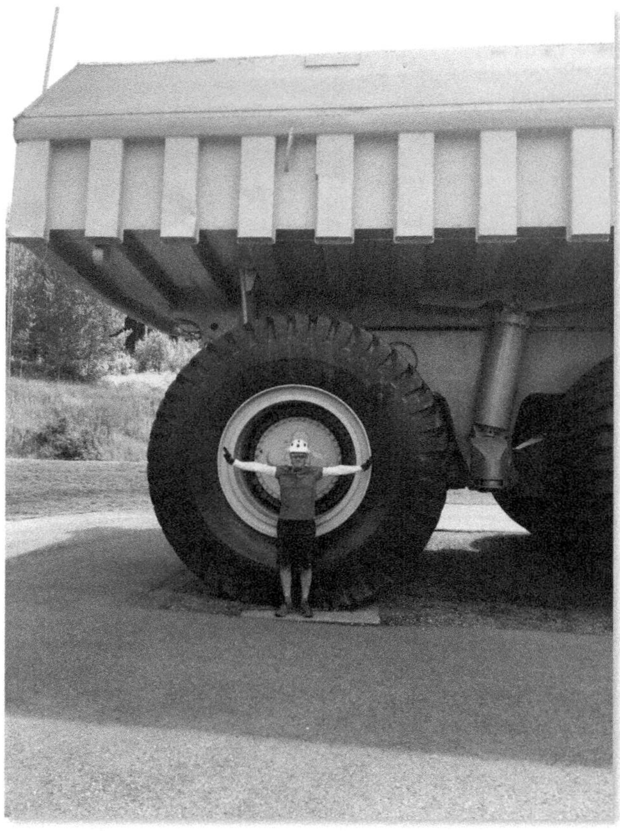

In the late afternoon we are biking on Highway 3 with tons of traffic, and the headwind hasn't dissipated. I notice we are biking hard and still only moving at eight miles per hour. When you bike that slowly for long stretches, you feel like you are never going to get to your destination. I know this is a journey, and that we will encounter many different terrains throughout, but biking on the side of a busy road with cars is not my idea of being with nature.

Eventually, we roll into the small town of Fernie. There is a local ski mountain, and it's absolutely stunning. As we ride into town I wave at the cargo train which is slowly passing us. The driver toots his horn as he rolls by. My in-laws, John and Tashia, who have road-biked across the country, have a commissioned painting of their trip—with the two of them on their bikes and a train in the background. We have been admiring the painting for years, and seeing this one brings back fond memories that John and Tashia have shared with us over the years—and which we, too, will now have. Our encounter with today's train creates a very special moment for us.

John says he feels "like the luckiest guy on the planet to be walking [biking] in his parents' footsteps." It's quite an honor.

We check in to the Best Western, which happens to have laundry. So, for the first time in three days, we will have clean clothes. The girl at the front desk can clearly see where we are coming from. She gives us a room right next to the laundry machines, exchanges my money for quarters, and gives me free laundry soap for the washer.

Our room is huge compared to the inside of our tent. We are able to unpack, roll out, and dry out our tent from the first night's rain. It's amazing what you take for granted when you don't have a warm bed, hot shower, and laundry.

It's glorious to sleep two days in a row in a real bed. This is turning out to be much more comfortable than I had originally imagined. It's making me more motivated to go further each day so that we can reach towns with hotels and services, rather than pitch a tent.

We dine at a local pizza place (if you can't tell by now that I love pizza, then I don't know what to say), and I order enough food to take on the trail for the next day.

Ending day stats:

Start 9:00 a.m. Finish 4:50 p.m.
7 hours and 50 minutes
52.26 miles

GDMBR Day 4
July 20, Wednesday

Weather—Sunny, hot
Fernie, Canada, to Eureka, MT, USA

John's Notes: Eureka, although a long way down the road, has full services. Carrie and I decide to push for the services.

America, here we come!

The breakfast spread at the Best Western is beyond grand and a great way to start the morning for our travels back to the United States. The road is long, hot, and paved, and the past two days have had far more pavement and speeding cars than we were hoping for. The rural country roads are much more enjoyable.

Ever since we left, I make a conscious effort to be present for each hour of our ride. Some days my mind wanders back to the beauty and challenges of Canada. Today at 3:20 p.m. we get in line at US Customs to re-enter the United States, and John proudly attaches his American flag to the front of his bike as we ride over the border from Canada into the United States.

In the past six hours we have biked from the small hilly ski town of Fernie to the rolling hills and open farms of Montana. There is a regular theme to the landscape on today's ride. Montana farms all proudly have a US flag or an eagle on their mailboxes, and there are a lot of horses, cows, and goats. By the late afternoon it is incredibly hot, so we are happy when we roll into Eureka—our final goal for the day.

Trail magic appears again today. The motel owner was telling me that just yesterday all of their rooms had been sold out, and that we would have had to camp across the street. Within walking distance from our hotel we are able to find a great vegan dinner, with a glass of wine, no less, at the local casino. The 4 Corners Casino and Crossroads Grill turns out to be one of the finest restaurants we'll encounter on the trip—both dinner and breakfast are amazing, and we are able to stock up at the gas station for the next couple of days as well. There is not much fresh food, but they have a Subway, and we are finding that a footlong on the trail is enough food for an entire day.

Ending day stats:

Start 7:50 a.m. Finish 7:25 p.m.
11 hours and 35 minutes
65.12 miles

The Trail
Montana

GDMBR Day 5
July 21, Thursday

Weather—Sunny, hot
Eureka to Red Meadow Lake Campground, MT

John's Notes: Whitefish was all uphill and out of reach in a single day, so a night out camping was our goal.

If you don't think it's about the miles, know this:
It's always about the miles.

The route today takes us from rural homes and farms to a national forest, and it's nice to ride alongside a beautiful river. The first 30 miles of the trail feel odd because we are riding in the forest but on a newly paved road, and it seems out of place in the middle of nature. Once the paved road turns to dirt it becomes a much harder climb, and we kind of wish we could continue traveling on pavement for the rest of the day.

Our first small goal of the day is to have lunch at a campsite called Tuchuk. After climbing for four hours I am starving, and I know I won't make it. We pull off to the side and eat our lunch near a natural mountain stream.

After lunch we come across the Ford Cabin, which has river access, so we are able to take a much-needed dip in the stream. The river is wide and shallow, and just deep enough for us to get completely submerged, so we are able to enjoy a cold dunk for our tired and sore muscles.

Beyond the river, our map indicates we will have a long hill climb from the Ford Cabin to Red Meadow Campground. At 5:00 p.m. we turn onto the final road with just 12 miles to go. Unfortunately, all 12 miles are straight uphill! With the sun in our faces, a low water supply, and an onslaught of horse flies and mosquitoes, the uphill climb is even harder.

At 6:30 p.m. we are still not close to the top, so we pull over to share the second half of my wilted Subway sandwich. We are also completely out of water, so we find a cold stream and, for the first time on the trip, we purify our water.

The sun continues to pound our faces, and our bodies begin to wither from the tough climbing, the heat of the sun, and the relentless attack of mosquitos. John patiently and kindly coaches me up the hill, reminding me of the small number of miles we have left. We are only on day five, yet mentally and physically I am feeling depleted. It's difficult to imagine keeping this pace for another 55 days.

At 7:20 p.m., nearly 12 hours after leaving Eureka, we finally reach our campsite. We quickly find an empty lakeside campsite which includes a bear box. John and I pitch the tent and start a campfire. The mosquitos make their assault, but we have our head nets. I cook a modest and quick dinner on the campfire, consisting of two bean-and-cheese burritos that I grabbed from the gas station in Eureka.

At 3:30 a.m. the skies open up, and it rains hard. At 5:30 a.m. hail comes down hard on our little tent, sometimes hitting me in the head because I am too close to the tent wall. We wake up very early, feeling quite cold, with several inches of hail surrounding our tent. A local fisherman, who is at the next campsite over, tells us we missed the moose and its baby swimming across the pond last night as the sun set. It would have been such a treat to see that, but neither of us had any energy left to stay up once we ate dinner.

Ending day stats:

Start 7:50 a.m. Finish 7:25 p.m.
11 hours and 35 minutes
65.12 miles

GDMBR Day 6
July 22, Friday

Weather—Cold hail, rain, and sun
Red Meadow Lake to Whitefish, MT

John's Notes: Our intent was to ride more than 30.26 miles, but after five hard days, as we passed the Whitefish Hotel and Spa, we found ourselves turning in with a smile.

When the road is hard, take a breath.

Our day starts in the freezing cold; in fact, I have three jackets on. My legs are so sore from the long day before, and I tell John I am not sure how far I can go today. As we start to descend, John mentions that he isn't sure if we are going the right way. Wait, what? The hill continues down, and down, and down. The descent is a great break from the hill climb we did yesterday. But we aren't sure if it's the right direction; if we have to turn around, I am going to have a fit.

By 10:00 a.m. the sun's warmth is enough to shed some layers of clothing, and we pass a trail marker that finally confirms our downhill direction is the right pathway. We both feel relieved. We take the downhill as our reward for the prior day's 12-mile hill climb—our bikes do weigh 75 pounds, after all, so hill climbing is not as easy as it is on a road bike or a traditional mountain bike.

There is more downhill throughout most of the morning, and when we hit the pavement we are catapulted from dirty ragamuffin trail riders into the lifestyles of the rich and the famous. The homes on Whitefish Lake are huge and beautiful. We are stinky, sore, hungry, and filthy. I am beginning to be proud of the way I look, as I know how far I have already come to get to Whitefish—and for me, this is a huge accomplishment.

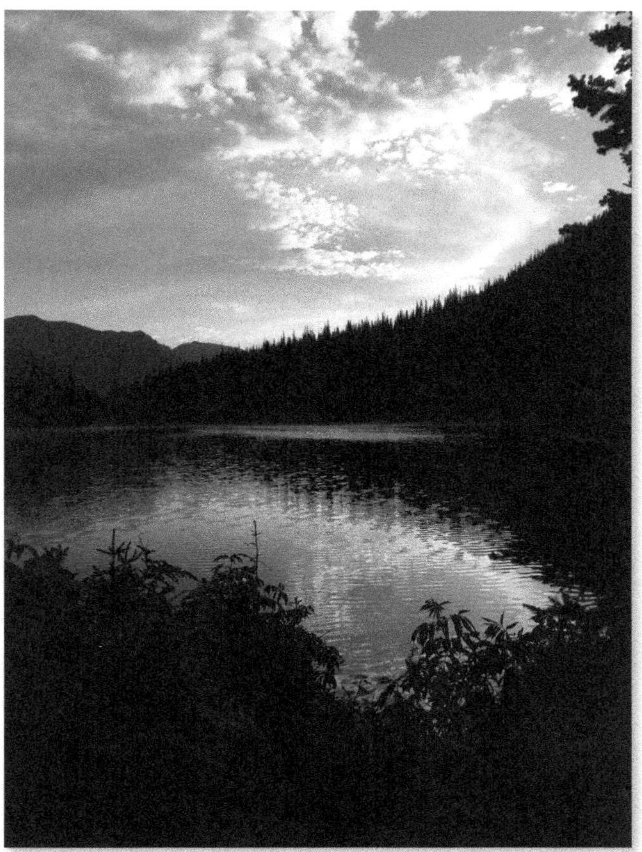

We stay on the paved road for the next 10 miles with the majestic lake as our view, and soon my secret prayer is answered by a lodge and spa on the water. As we pull into the resort, a seaplane lands, and a bride-to-be gets out, joining her family and guests who are excited to celebrate her union with her husband-to-be. This place is beyond picturesque, and we both really enjoy witnessing the seaplane landing.

The hotel doesn't have any regular rooms available, but we are able to rent a condo by the lake and gladly take it. Once we check in and unpack, I immediately start laundry, take a shower, and head out to the grand deck where we are greeted with a huge menu for lunch.

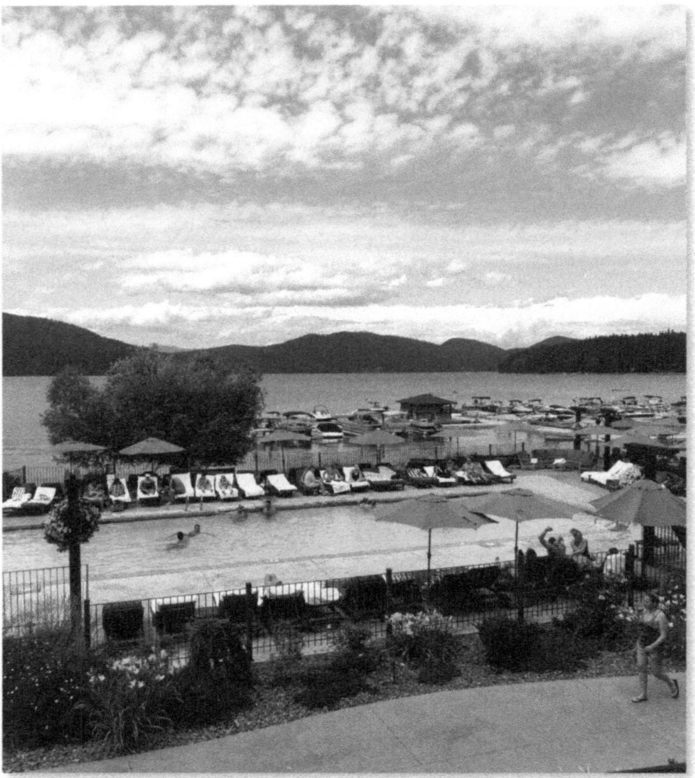

As vegans, we are delighted because the hotel has great meatless- and dairy-free options. We order the TLT—a tempeh, lettuce & tomato sandwich—the vegan equivalent of a BLT. However, they accidentally deliver our TLT to the young kids at the table next to us. We watch their faces as their wrinkled-up noses and totally gross looks come after just one bite. We knew what must have happened, and we have a great laugh. Tempeh, we admit, is an acquired taste—especially if you were expecting bacon. The father of the children wasn't paying much attention and it looks just like a BLT, so he tells them to eat it!

Instead of getting involved, I quietly tell our waiter what's happened, and he immediately makes things better for the two kids.

After lunch, we are able to get massages, which I know will be extremely helpful for our overworked bodies. My mind needs a break, too, because we have been riding really hard, and it's starting to take a toll. At the current pace, I am starting to question whether or not I can make the entire trip. We are only on day six.

After a relaxing massage and a long afternoon nap, I try to open my laptop to write my blog, and it dies. No, it does not simply run out of battery; it sputters its final breath and dies. Now I will have to type my daily blogs on my phone with one finger. Prior to this ride, having my computer crash would have been far more of an event than it was. My attitude has already changed—after just six days on the trail—and I finally feel I have made the transition to life on the GDMBR. I think to myself: *There is nothing you can do—take a breath, and it will be okay.*

Ending day stats:

Start 8:05 a.m. Finish 11:30 a.m.
3 hours and 25 minutes
30.26 miles

GDMBR Day 7
July 23, Saturday

Weather—Cool, overcast, sun
Whitefish to a river campsite, MT

John's Notes: With our wonderfully short and rejuvenating day yesterday, we are ready for the journey today. With no prospect for a warm bed and no shortage of miles, we put our heads down and crank out the miles.

To reach the finish line, sometimes you have to recharge your own batteries.

We start our morning with rested legs and watch a mama duck and her babies walk across the morning grass, each blade sprinkled with shiny pindrops of dew.

At 7:54 a.m., we are out the door and on our way—the weather is cool and overcast, perfect for biking. Within an hour we reach the city limits of Whitefish and begin biking the back roads of rural farmland. A few miles into the trail, John spots our first and only bear of the trip. I never see the bear, and I am not upset that I missed it.

Most of the farms are spread out and modest, which makes for a stark contrast when we bike past a wealthy ranch. These farms, or estates, have large fences, big gates, and "no trespassing" signs posted all around.

We are able to bike in the rolling hills at a pretty good pace, biking 40 miles by lunchtime. We do take one wrong turn, but we are only off course for a mile or two. We stop at a lemonade stand and support a budding young entrepreneur while enjoying a nice conversation with the young girl and her grandpa. We ask questions about their community and her future goals as we sip down the cool drinks.

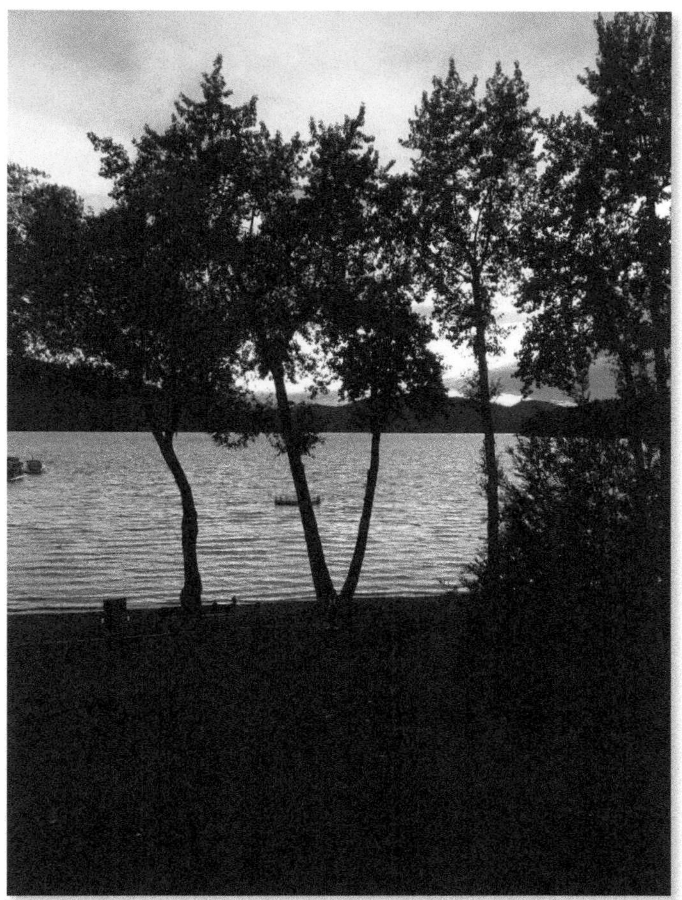

For lunch we find a popular local spot on the trail—Echo Lake Cafe. This little gem has wonderful home-cooked food, which makes it hard for us to keep to our plant-based and pescatarian diet. Luckily, we are able to resist the more appealing foods, and I am still able to indulge in a freshly cooked tuna sandwich that's paired with a spinach salad. John has a black bean burrito with veggie potatoes. We order some more potatoes to go, and I take half my tuna sandwich in a box because both will be perfect for dinner tonight. Many of the cafe patrons want to talk with us, and some share their own desires to bike part, or all, of the trail—of course, we encourage them to give it a go.

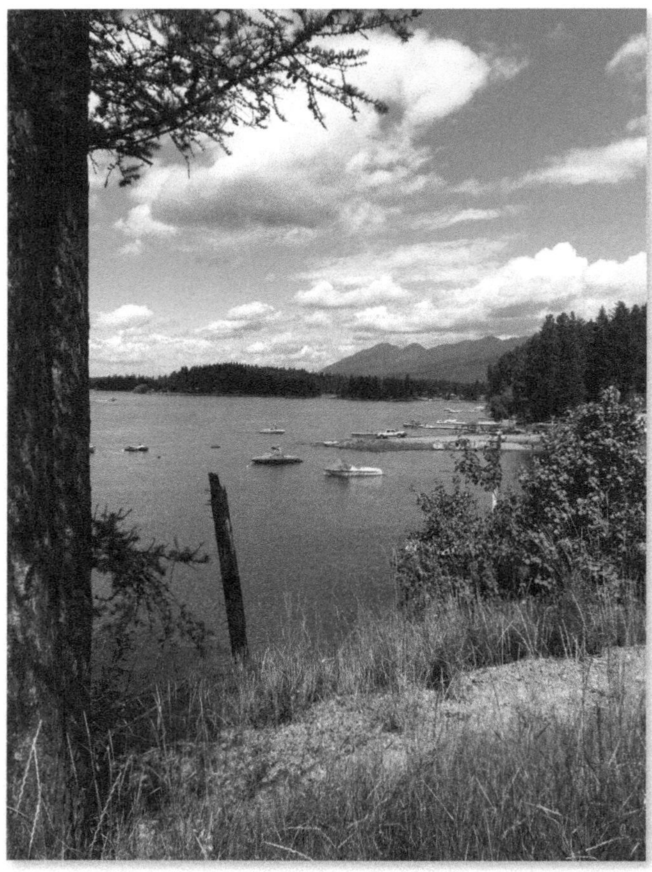

By 3:00 p.m. the dirt road turns into a six-mile climb on a logging road. It takes us one and a half hours to climb it, but the sun is kept at bay by the dense trees that surround the trail. The break we took in Whitefish totally refreshed my legs, and the hill climb doesn't hurt as much. From a mental standpoint, it's great to get 40 miles in before lunch, as we now have only 20 miles remaining for the day—or so we think.

By early evening my cyclometer says we've gone 75 miles for the day, and we both start to get concerned about finding the unmarked campsite because we are now 15 miles past the 60 miles we originally planned for—and none of the turns we make feel right. We reach a fork in the road, and John makes the decision to turn right—basing his decision on the turn-by-turn sheets attached to his handlebars. When we reach the main road, however, we realize we have passed the campsite, so we quickly turn back and find the campsite on the river. Another GDMBR couple is here—from France, with a baby in tow. A local couple is camping here too, and they are quite friendly, offering us appetizers and dessert. Their dog, Max, is a welcome treat as well, because we have not seen our dog, Nina, in over 10 days. Max is a German shorthaired pointer and loves to play stick, just like Nina.

It generally takes us about an hour to set up camp—to pitch our tent, make our bed, unpack our panniers, change into our night clothes, build a campfire, and cook dinner. This particular day we were on the trail for almost 12 hours—the actual pedaling time was close to 9 hours—so our bodies are simply exhausted, and bedtime cannot arrive soon enough to satisfy us.

A note for campers: When camping next to or close to a river, your tent will be weighed down by dew in the morning. If you have time, and if there is sunshine, dry your tent before you pack up. A wet tent means a significant increase in weight on your bike and an inevitably more difficult ride as a result.

Ending day stats:

Start 7:50 a.m. Finish 7:20 p.m.
11 hours and 30 minutes
79.55 miles

GDMBR Day 8
July 24, Sunday

End of week one
Weather—Sun, hot
A river campsite to Holland Lake Lodge, MT

John's Notes: Our intent is to have lunch at Holland Lake Lodge and continue another 40 miles to Seeley Lake, where there will be a hotel and the luxury of a hot shower and a soft bed, which will give us a chance to recharge our batteries.

Waking up on the river is magical.

Fresh air, sounds of rushing water, and the crisp, cool temperatures make for the perfect alarm clock. Bears did not visit our campsite last night, which makes all three groups of campers very happy. The dew on the tent is abundant, and John works hard to get it off our tent before we roll it up and put it in our pannier. As a result, we get a later start than we had originally hoped for. The streams we encounter on the start of the ride are majestic, and the green and vibrant moss on the banks makes the water starkly white as it flows down the hill.

As we start our climb, my legs resist and pedaling becomes quite the task. They hurt so bad from the day before, and all I can think about is Holland Lake for lunch and Seeley Lake for dinner. But as the hill continues, my attitude sours. What am I doing? Why am I pushing so hard?

Is this trip even fun? We have been gone only one week, and each day we find ourselves pushing our bodies harder than the day before. We just put our heads down and grind until our bodies are at sheer exhaustion. Is this the kind of trip we signed up for? The questions and self-doubts continue to roll in.

Still, the view as we approach Holland Lake Lodge is gorgeous, much like a view in our home state of Colorado. The lake is surrounded by snow-capped peaks, with green grass in the valley and an abundance of colorful wildflowers.

But even this beauty isn't enough to quash my doubts, and the questions arise again. It's already 2:00 p.m. in the afternoon, and we haven't traveled as far as we'd wanted to.

I ask John, "Is this fun for you?"

The question sparks a tearful conversation for me. I just don't know how much further I can go. Even with all the Ironman races I've completed, I have never done them day after day like this. John sees that I am really struggling both physically and mentally, and he agrees to slow down and modify our daily goal. I want to take a little more time to enjoy our surroundings, and I believe (I hope!) slowing down will increase the likelihood of reaching our final goal of Antelope Wells, New Mexico—which right now seems like a long way off. We decide to make Holland Lake Lodge our stop for the night.

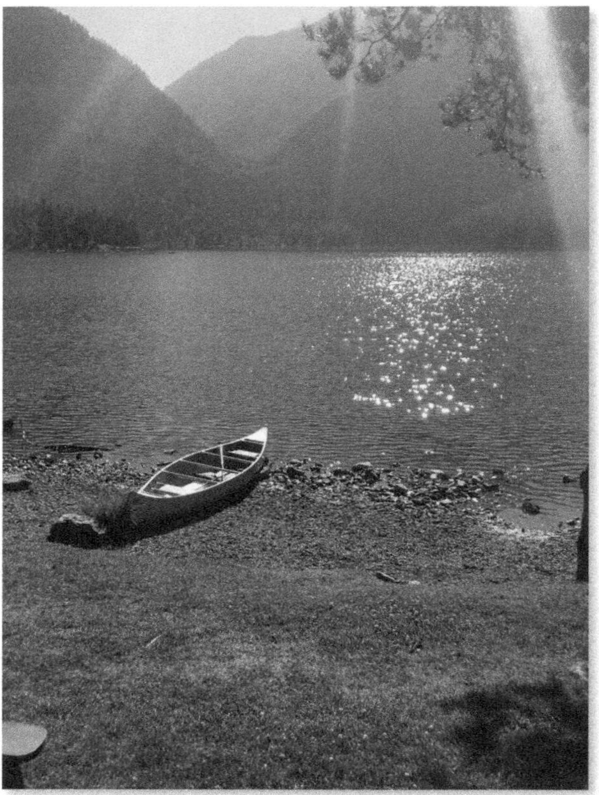

Our original plan was to get to the lodge in time to have lunch, so I am not carrying much food in my pannier. There is absolutely no reason to carry the extra weight of food when we know we'll be eating at a restaurant later. Unfortunately, after checking in at the Holland Lake

Lodge, we are informed that we haven't made it in time for lunch—we missed it by a half hour.

I almost cry.

Our host senses my sadness and offers to make us sandwiches. Even though we don't normally eat cheese, we do not hesitate when two cheese-and-lettuce sandwiches arrive. In fact, they are the best sandwiches we can ever remember eating. We are also so parched that we drink 10 sparkling waters between the two of us. An afternoon at the rustic Holland Lake Lodge, sipping sparkling waters, is the pace I need. And, after our two-hour nap, we head to the beach area to enjoy a swim in the lake.

The Montana resort is a place where you find families gathering to enjoy summer weather and activities. The kids are running around on the expansive grass and swimming with the local lodge dog, Willie, a short and fat golden retriever that loves swimming, fishing, and playing with kids. This creates a sense of belonging for John and me that we have been missing on the trip.

At one point, Willie jumps on a stand-up paddleboard with a guest and insists that they go looking for fish. He stands at the helm and guides his guest rider toward his favorite fishing spot. When Willie is done, he simply jumps off the SUP board and runs directly over to me. He shakes off the lake water and lies down on my beach towel to dry his body. He is upside down, and taking complete advantage of my towel. This makes me laugh so hard—what a joy it is be here!—and I understand this is exactly the mental break I need.

We head back to our room to get ready for dinner. Both John and I have only one outfit for after biking, and so far it has been working out well. I have black leggings and a black tank top, with a plaid button-down and a black Patagonia skirt. John has one pair of technical pants, an Under Armour short-sleeve shirt, and long-sleeve zip-collar shirt.

For dinner, we sit at the huge picture window and watch the kids chase each other on the lawn. The evening birds come out and feast on worms, moths, and other small flying edibles.

I am so happy that we didn't push through the day. It's been great to recalibrate our pace and work toward ensuring we complete the entire 2,800-mile adventure. It takes us a while to realize that the GDMBR is as much about mental toughness as it is physical.

Ending day stats:

Start 8:50 a.m. Finish 2:20 p.m.
5 hours and 30 minutes
40.79 miles

GDMBR Day 9
July 25, Monday

Weather—Sun, hot
Holland Lake to Seeley Lake, MT

John's Notes: The climb to Seeley Lake is 2500 feet, and the journey is not easy. When we left Banff we thought we would have to camp more often. Rolling into Seeley Lake offers another soft bed and warm shower. Our objective is to complete the GDMBR, and not use a rock for a pillow.

You can only succeed if you try.

We wake up feeling renewed, and we snuggle together under a soft, oversized down comforter. The swallows just outside our window are feeding their hungry babies. This is the kind of magical morning we need to inspire us to keep on riding. The sun is sparkling on the lake, making it look like a diamond in the sunlight. The temperature is already warm, which will set the theme for the day: *hot!* Breakfast service doesn't start until 8:30 a.m., so we are forced to take our time getting ready because breakfast is a *must* for us.

With a renewed pace, we decide to enjoy our first stop of the day at Clearwater Lake for lunch, and a swim to boot. It is a pristine, clear green-bottom lake nestled in the mountains. While we are enjoying a swim in the lake, we see three loons doing the same! As we are eating our lunch, we meet a couple who are picking up trash. They are about my parents' ages. We find out they have left Florida to enjoy retirement in Montana. They volunteer once a month for the US Forest Service to clean up the trails.

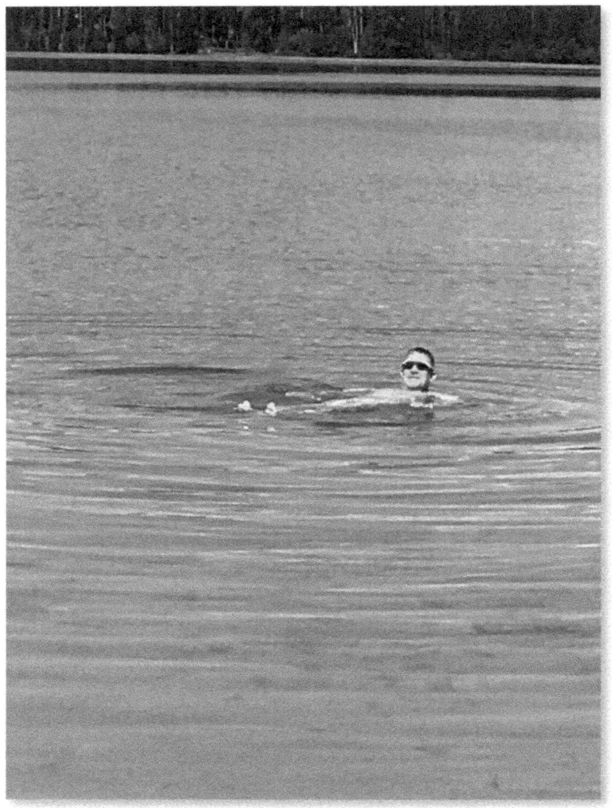

After lunch we continue to climb. We pass the French couple and their baby, with whom we shared a campground two nights ago. They tell us the night before they camped next to our Holland Lake Lodge, enjoyed a swim in that crisp lake, and were able to stock up on some food.

About four miles up from Clearwater Lake a family in a van with young rambunctious boys asks us for directions to Clearwater Lake. They had passed it a ways back, so we give them directions to head back to where they came from. They ask about our journey and say, "Why would you do such a thing?" The mother asks our names, and says "John and Carrie, you are now in our prayers." This is an example of the kind of warmth and love we receive from so many people on the trail. I consider telling her she is in my prayers, being in charge of all those energetic boys. But I don't want her to take it the wrong way, so I just smile and say, "Thank you."

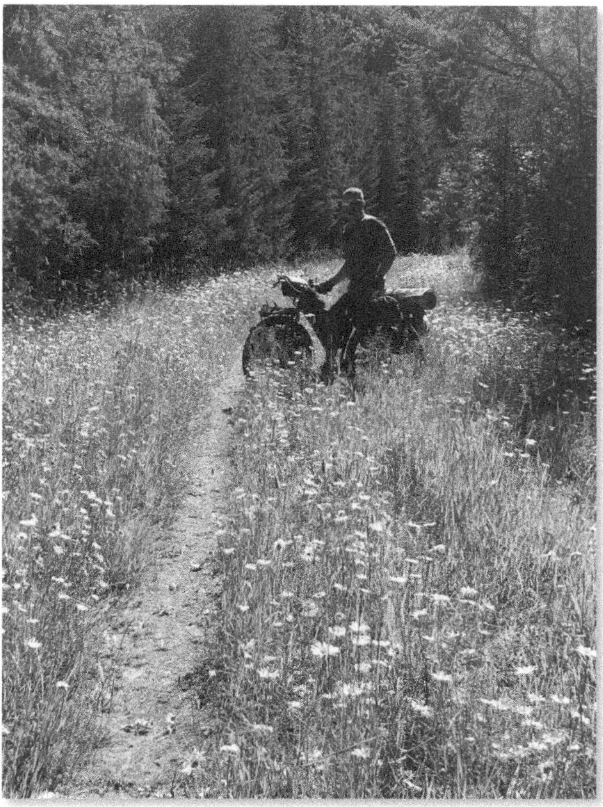

Our climb soon turns into a single-track trail laden—adorned—with wild daisies. At the summit, the view is filled with pink wildflowers, tall pine trees, and in the far distance we can see the snow-capped mountains that we crossed over just a couple of days ago. Farther up the summit we will easily see Clearwater Lake, but from here it's just a faraway pond.

Shortly after summiting, we go through a fire field—which is just what it sounds like, a field that has gone through a massive fire—that must have happened a few years back. We can see and feel how forest fires can change ecosystems. Although a towering forest was gone, already a new forest of small saplings was taking a foothold. Forest fires are one of the many challenges of the GDMBR. Every year there seems to be at least one diversion on the trail because of a forest fire.

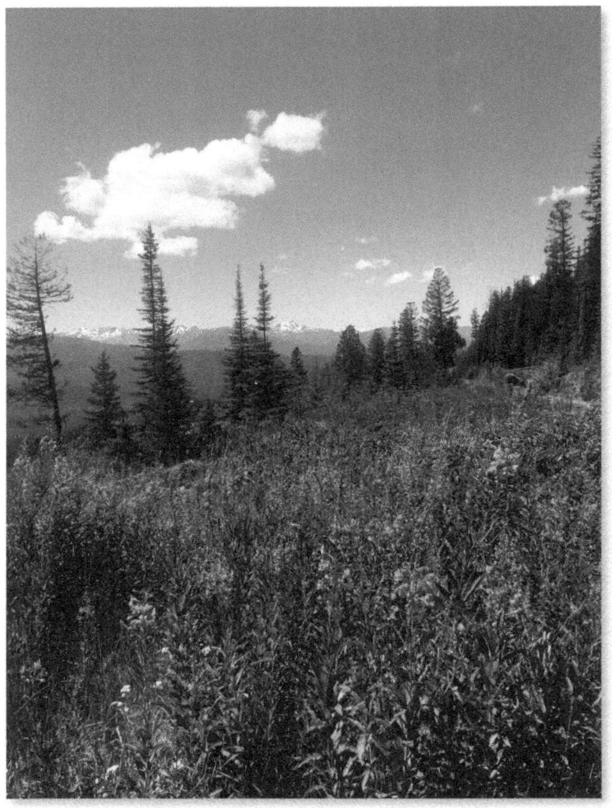

As we roll into Seeley Lake, we discover a hotel right on the trail and decide to stay there. After a hot shower we bike our way into town. There is one grocery store and three restaurants: a steakhouse, a chicken restaurant, and a restaurant in a casino. We choose the steakhouse first, as it has a nice view at the top of the hill, and generally we are able to find a nice piece of fish and a plain baked potato when we dine at steakhouses. This was not to be the case in Montana, however.

We are seated for dinner and the menu is delivered to our table. They have three cuts of beef served four ways: rare, medium rare, medium well, and well done. There are no salads and no side dishes. It's truly a steakhouse that serves only steak. Our waitress tells us that we can find a garden burger (vegan, made from beans and veggies) from the burger truck at the bottom of the hill—but that's not exactly the sit-down dinner we have been anticipating. So we move on to the chicken restaurant.

Where they serve . . . only chicken.

So, hoping the third time's a charm, we head to the casino. Everything on the menu is fried, and the indoor ambiance—or lack thereof—has us thinking the garden burger outside on the lake seems just right. When leaving the casino, we run into Jake, the fellow GDMBRer, traveling alone, whom we met at the pizza place in Elkford, Canada.

Something is up because Jake is crying. He tells us he is quitting the ride and trying to hitch a ride to Missoula to catch a bus home. It's nearly a 30-hour bus ride from Missoula to Kansas City. We insist that Jake come with us and try a garden burger from the burger truck. The setting is beautiful and the food is not too bad. We try to convince Jake to bike with us for a few days, but he has made his decision to head home.

Jake has just graduated college and biking the GDMBR has been his dream; unfortunately, his knees will not let him continue.

John tells him, "You only fail if you never try."

Jake replies that he has given the GDMBR his best effort. While we are eating, we talk about life and how Jake should try the GDMBR again when he has a partner to bike with. John and I tell him that we've been discovering it's easier to handle the mental toughness of the route if you can share it with someone you love—or at least like to spend time with. We tell him about my meltdown from the day before—which, frankly, I had not seen coming—and how it forced us to regroup and reevaluate the massive miles we were taking on.

Because he is on a "just-graduated-college budget," Jake had been trying to do as many miles a day as possible and couldn't afford to stay in hotels, get a hot shower, and grab a good night's sleep. His diet consisted of eating candy bars and drinking soda—maybe cheap, but not sustainable. All of this was taking its toll on his body.

After we say goodbye, we never see Jake again.

Ending day stats:

Start 9:30 a.m. Finish 4:20 p.m.
6 hours and 50 minutes
40.9 miles

GDMBR Day 10
July 26, Tuesday

Weather—Sun, cool to warm
Seeley Lake to Lincoln, MT

John's Notes: Helena was our next day's goal, and moving from hotel to hotel was starting to feel right for us. To think that GDMBR racers roll into Helena after only a few days of riding and sleeping on the side of the road—they are superhuman.

It's always about the miles!

The morning ride starts with a beautiful uphill climb. We are the only ones on the dirt road, and the sun is shining bright.

We make it to the summit; lunch cannot come soon enough. Luckily, we are close to lunchtime when we roll into the small town of Ovando.

Ovando is directly on the trail and has a great restaurant famous to the GDMBR—The Stray Bullet Cafe! We see a single touring mountain bike just outside the Stray Bullet, and when we get inside the cafe I notice the rider from the day before. He was in Seeley Lake when we were, but he never stopped to say hi or chat—which is not the GDMBR way. I go over to say hello to him and ask how far he is going, but he never gives me a straight answer. This is a huge red flag. Bikers should be wary when they encounter other bikers behaving this way. When a GDMBR rider can't answer where they are going or how far they have gone, or which town is next, there is a problem.

We sit down and eat a delicious lunch, then head on our way—the lone cycler stays when we leave. When we get back on the road, I can't stop thinking about that guy. I had recognized him from when we were leaving Clearwater Lake, because he passed us heading north, and now he was headed south! This seemed very strange to me.

The questions start rattling through my mind, and it's all I can talk about for the next few hours: What would we do if the cycler was following us and wanted to hurt us? The mind is a powerful thing, and I realize I'm beginning to psych myself out.

Just then John comes up with an answer that has some potential. What if the lone cycler dropped out of the GDMBR trail, but because he'd already taken time off from work, he decided to keep at it by doing sections of the trail each day?

Whatever the reason for this guy's odd actions, we don't see him again. And I eventually dial back my worst-case thinking.

We get to the base of the pass at 3:00 p.m., which is also the peak heat of the day. It is so hot that we decide to go for a skinny dip (sorry, no photo) in the Dry Creek. We hide under the bridge so the cars can't see us. The water is runoff from melting snow, and it's cold! We sit down and soak for as long as possible in the freezing water. This is just the physical therapy we need. Now it's time for the second big climb of the day.

When we reach Arrastra Creek, on the top of the next big hill climb, we get off our bikes and take some time to enjoy the creek, as its beauty is well worth the short stop. From Helena National Forest, the rest of the day is a downhill trek.

After being in the saddle for over eight hours, Lincoln is a warm welcome. We choose the first hotel that pops up on my Yelp search; it's called Leepers. When we pull in, we are greeted by several dogs and horses. I enjoy a face-lick from an Australian shepherd, who in turn enjoys all the salt from my face. Nina, our dog back home, is a mini Australian shepherd, and we miss her terribly. As a result, anytime we run into a dog on the trek, we don't hesitate to share belly scratches and face licks.

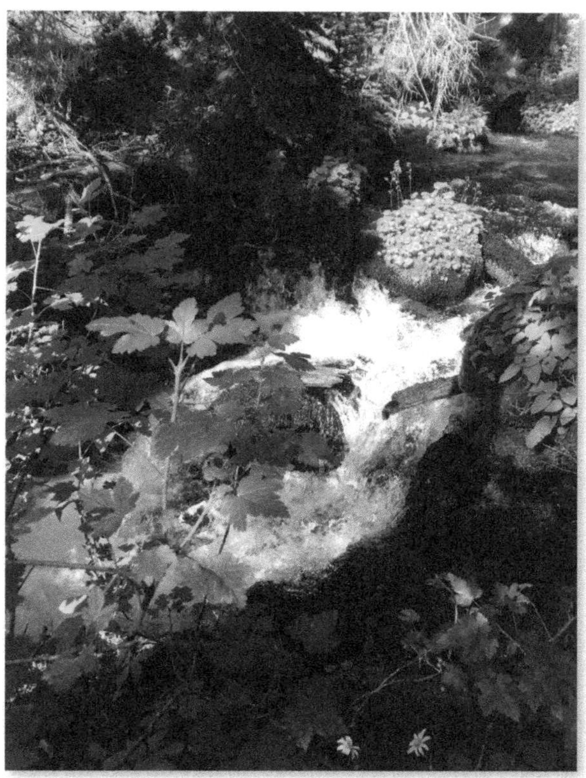

I know this trip is about the journey—drinking from a cool mountain stream, cresting a hill and taking in an incredible vista, getting licks from a friendly dog after a long ride, etc. But most days it has to be about the miles. The miles are how we measure for our food, water, accommodations for the night, and laundry. While we would love to end each day of riding at 5:00 p.m., it's the miles and the sleeping accommodations or campgrounds that dictate our finish line. By the time we get into Lincoln, it's 6:20 p.m., and after unpacking showering and doing laundry, it's 8:00 and we haven't even had dinner. So we hustle to one of the local casinos for a bite to eat.

Montana has a vibrant casino industry, and it seems as if every restaurant is also a casino. These aren't like the Las Vegas casinos; they are more like a buffet at a gas station casino. We choose a less-smoke-filled casino for dinner tonight, and our waitress and cook are the salt of the earth. While we're ordering our dinner, our waitress informs us that the grocery store is only open until 8:30. She allows us to run over to the store and holds our dinner order until we get back.

We have to study the map quickly and figure out what we need for the next day. We know if we want to reach a hotel the next day in Helena, we will have three Continental Divide crossings to climb, so we need to stock up on food. This was especially important in case we didn't make it to Helena and instead had to camp.

After dinner, we hit the hay immediately.

Ending day stats:
Start 7:45 a.m. Finish 6:20 p.m.
10 hours and 35 minutes
67.97 miles

GDMBR Day 11
July 27, Wednesday

Weather—Sun, overcast, hail
Lincoln to Helena, MT

John's Notes: We had three Continental Divide crossings ahead of us, and knew that if we could make it to Helena, it would be well worth it. We also knew that the end of the day would bring a long downhill coast into Helena, so we were ready.

More in the tellin' than the doin'.

We knew it would be hard to start . . . but we didn't know it would be *this* hard! Our first crossing of the day on the Continental Divide is the hardest climb yet. We climb for about two hours before reaching a turn in the road that really tests my ability. As soon as we come around the corner, the only sights ahead are many more hills, with tough climbs that I know we'll have to ascend by pushing our bikes. Walking our bikes is one thing, but walking our bikes for more than two miles up such steep and rocky hills, fully loaded with the weight of our gear, is a totally different animal.

After quite a few hills, we pass the Empire Mine. I stop to take a photo and then I text it to John Farnam, a dear friend of ours in Colorado. He immediately texts back to say the Empire Mine is "on the back side of the Great Divide Ski Area," a place he grew up skiing as a little kid. It was previously known as the Belmont Ski Area for being located on Mount Belmont. It is particularly special for us to discover more about where John grew up because he is such a special friend to us.

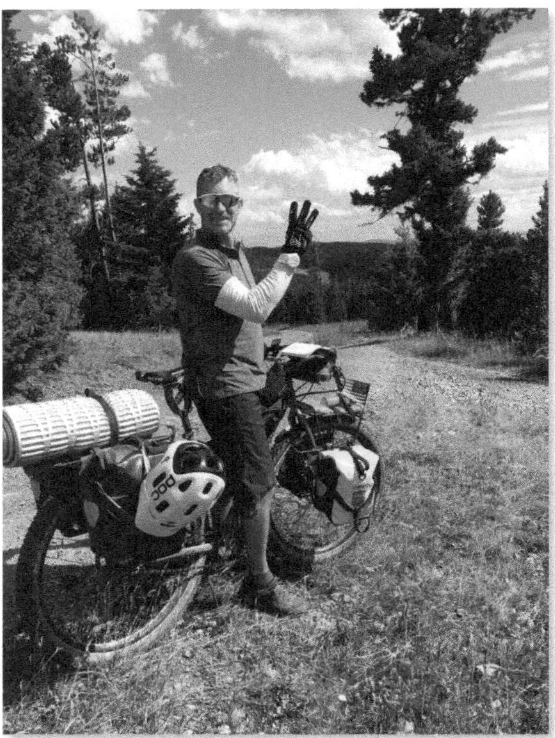

We press on.

There are two more Continental Divide Crossings left today. Time is beginning to run short, and we're still less than half way to Helena. After reaching the top of the second crossing, some Great Divide motorcycle riders stop to check on us. They tell us about their journey and their inevitable breakdowns, while John and I pass along the joys and challenges of our journey. One of the motorcyclists tells us that he'd really like to do the route again on a mountain bike like us. We tell him that we would really like to do the route again, but next time on a motorcycle.

We say our goodbyes and hit the road again, both of us sharing the same journey but at very different speeds.

Then the hail comes . . .

Foul weather when crossing high Continental Divide passes is always a concern. When the flash of lightning and the crack of thunder are simultaneous, and you can feel the static electricity in the air, you know it's time to head for cover.

Luckily, we are safely off the summit as the hail starts to fall. We are actually happy about the hail because it's better than getting soaked in the rain. Still, it is coming down pretty hard and in rather big chunks. John and I have to tuck our legs underneath the crossbar of our bikes in order to avoid getting pelted by hail. Eventually it starts coming down too hard for us to continue biking, so we find shelter under a small tree, which of course only delays our journey that much more.

At 5:00 p.m. we are still climbing and have biked only 40 miles. I start to wonder how much farther I can go.

Slowly I realize I'm headed for another breakdown. I know it's from a lack of food, a long day, and the reality that we are still 25 long miles from Helena. And I know it's a classic example of how important it is to maintain mental fortitude on an undertaking like this.

So we stop for a snack, even though all I have in my pannier is a can of corn and some peach Crystal Light tea. As I fill my stomach I also replenish my resolve. Next to our picnic spot, the cows moo and the scent of pine trees fill the air.

Onward.

It's now 6:30 p.m., and summit number three is just around the corner. We have been climbing at four to five miles per hour, and if we keep this pace, we won't make it to Helena until 9:00 p.m.

We eventually reach what we think is the top of the third summit, but it just turns out to be a false summit, which is so demoralizing. Still, we are on the final hill, and there is nowhere else to go. I just keep my legs spinning, one turn at a time. We finally reach the summit, and the greatest blessing is in store for us—the remainder of the ride into Helena is downhill. Thirteen miles later, at 7:45 p.m., we arrive in Helena.

My father-in-law has this saying, "Some days there is more in the doin' than the tellin'. Other days there is more in the tellin' than in the doin'." Today there is "more in the tellin'." We certainly put our heads down and got the job done. But it was also a heck of a day: 65 miles, three Continental Divide crossings, and a hail storm.

Our night ends at the Best Western, where kind employees welcome us and warm cookies are waiting for us on the counter. Curious looks and stares from other hotel guests are inevitable—here and everywhere else we plop down for the night. We are always surprised that even some of the locals don't realize that the longest, toughest mountain bike route in North America goes through their own town.

Ending day stats:

Start 8:20 a.m. Finish 7:45 p.m.
11 hours and 25 minutes
64.53 miles

GDMBR Day 12
July 28, Thursday

Weather—Sun
Helena to Basin, MT

John's Notes: After such a long, hard slog the day before, we decided that trying to get to Butte, almost 83 miles of tough terrain, seemed like too much. The small town of Basin was just over 40 miles away and held the possibility of a hotel.

Don't be fooled by low miles.

When we looked at the mileage map last night, it looked like today would be an easy day. But we know there are no easy days on the GDMBR.

I dread getting out of bed and back in the saddle for another day, and I think John feels the same. He got up early to get some Epsom salt, and we both soak our bodies in the bathtub, to alleviate some of the soreness in our bodies before getting on the trail.

Before we can depart Helena, we also need to restock our supplies of food. At the local grocery store we bump into three other GDMBR riders. One rider we immediately recognize. He is the guy from France whom we had met in Banff at the grocery store. It's crazy to think that 600 miles later our paths would cross again in a grocery store.

After leaving the store, we begin our day with a three-hour hill climb.

We conquer it, and feel pretty good about ourselves and the rest of the day's journey, We have no idea how difficult the trail is about to get.

At 3:00 p.m. we start to climb on single track up Lava Mountain. The trail is steep and washed out, like a rocky riverbed, with downed trees, rocks, and ruts. We are unable to ride it and have to push our bikes instead. John's turn-by-turn directions indicate that we should reach the summit in a mile or so. As we push and lift and carry our bikes up the trail, it seems like we will never get there. I wonder how the racers handle this terrain at all hours of the day and night.

More than two hours later, at 5:00 p.m., we are still climbing Lava Mountain. We take a quick break and have a snack to regroup and regain our mental toughness. The stop gets us through the next hour, to the top of Lava Mountain. At last! But it's too steep for a stop. So we immediately head down the steep downhill—while Hoodoo Creek rages on our left—until we finally reach the bottom and our campsite for the night.

Tourists to Montana may know about the radon-filled Health Mines in this area outside Helena. Named for the supposed benefits received from low levels of radiation, the Health Mines attract visitors who believe spending time inside them is good for their health. But unless you're a local, you probably won't know that the campgrounds next to these mines are sometimes crowded by visiting Hutterites, an ethnoreligious group like the Amish, who make periodic pilgrimages to the mines.

There are four of these health mines in the United States, and all are located within 20 miles of one another in the Boulder-Basin area south of Helena. These mines are also only one of two locations in the entire world where radon is produced from the natural decay of uranium. The Hutterites, along with many others, believe that radon—although deadly in large doses—is actually a natural cure for chronic ailments. So every summer they come to the Basin to sit in the mines for their health.

Each family seems to have lots of kids. The girls and women all wear dresses and the boys and men all wear overalls. The Hutterite family camping next to us helps us find the campground pay box and offers wood for a fire while we set up camp.

Every family seems to have its own four-wheeler, which appears to be able to carry the entire family. There are two kids on the front, two kids on the back, and ma and pa in the middle. The camp is filled with laughter, kids playing, four-wheeler engine noise, and the sound of the river. After our difficult day, staying at such a great campsite feels like a real blessing.

Ending day stats:

Start 10:50 a.m. Finish 7:00 p.m.
7 hours and 50 minutes
43.58 miles

GDMBR Day 13
July 29, Friday

Weather—Sun, hot
Basin to Butte, MT

John's Notes: With Butte Montana, just 40 miles away, we decide a hotel stop is what we need.

Rough news to start the day.

Just before we leave the campsite, we get a call from our daughter, Michelle, who is crying. Our small dog, Nina, who is staying with Michelle and her boyfriend, Nate, and their two dogs, had gotten into a fight with one of their dogs and received a nasty bite on her neck. Michelle said they had already taken her to the emergency veterinarian, and that the vet was hopeful Nina would be okay—though the bite was so bad that the vet was going to have to stitch her neck up from the inside out. Nina was still in surgery when Michelle called, and there was nothing we could do but console our daughter. She was incredibly upset and we were sad for our dog. These things happen, though; we knew Michelle was doing everything she could.

We start our journey for the day hoping we will have cell service in order to receive updates on Nina. The day is already hot, and now with Nina in the hospital it has become mentally difficult. As we are leaving town, our daughter calls to give us good news about Nina. We are relieved and happy that our dog is out of surgery and already recovering.

The highlight of the day is summiting Continental Divide crossing #5. Every crossing brings us one crossing closer—out of 32 total—to our goal.

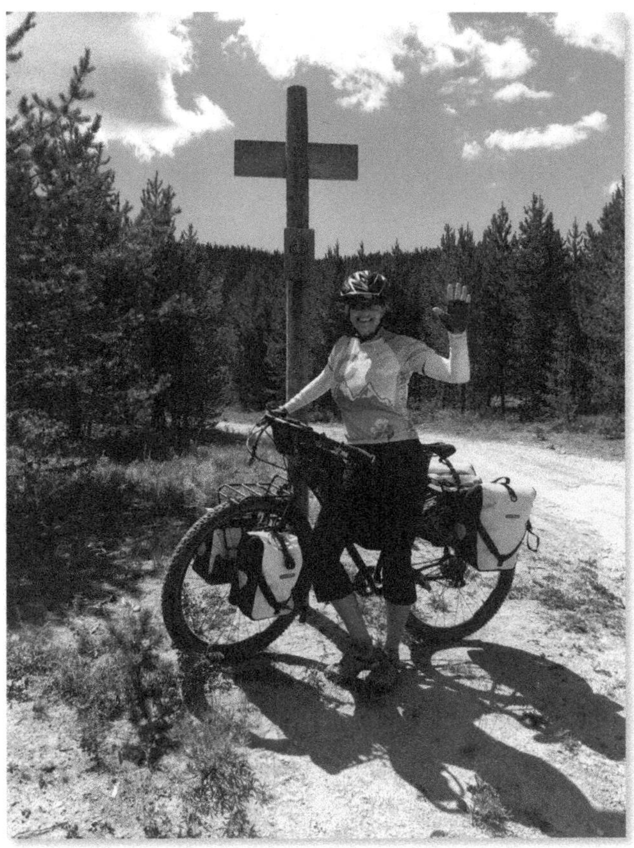

Before getting to Butte, which is to be our stop for the night, we ride by a small farm where a local artist displays some very cool metal sculptures along the fence line. Butte isn't far away by the time lunch rolls around, and although we had intended on making it to town before stopping, I just can't wait for lunch any longer. The only place to stop is on the busy paved road, and it's the only spot of shade we have seen in quite some time. John lays out the silver foam pad so we can sit down while we eat. Lunch is a can of soup, trail mix, and our beloved Crystal

Light packets with ice water. After lunch, it only takes us another hour and a half to reach the hotel.

We hit the hay shortly after we arrive, in preparation for an early start tomorrow. We are both starting to embody the mantra of the Great Divide Mountain Bike Route: eat, bike, sleep, repeat.

Ending day stats:

Start 8:00 a.m. Finish 2:15 p.m.
6 hours and 15 minutes
39.18 miles

GDMBR Day 14
July 30, Saturday

Weather—Sun, wind
Butte to Wise River Campground, MT

John's Notes: Wise River is our goal, some 60-plus mile away, but we still have the option to take the slightly shorter alternate route halfway through the day. The hotel accommodations in Wise River are questionable, but there are several camping options farther on.

Start wise, end wise.

We get off to an early start this morning and try to beat the heat. While doing laundry last night, I found my lightweight neck gaiter; I plan on using it to screen my chin and lips from the sun. The sun exposure is beginning to take its toll on every part of my bare skin. My chapped, swollen lips are certainly feeling the ill effects of the continuous exposure to the sun.

John's turn-by-turn for his cyclometer is slightly off, and it doesn't match his mapped-out turn-by-turn, so he has to add about two extra miles to his cyclometer before we can start the day. He rides around in the parking lot until we're ready to go. As we depart we get a reminder of yesterday's challenge when we look back and see the mountains we climbed over to get to Butte.

Today's journey starts off in a valley, and my legs feel so much better today after yesterday's nice long rest. We ride under one of the most beautiful train trestles I have ever encountered. It's long, sturdy, and a reminder that even manmade structures can look beautiful amid nature.

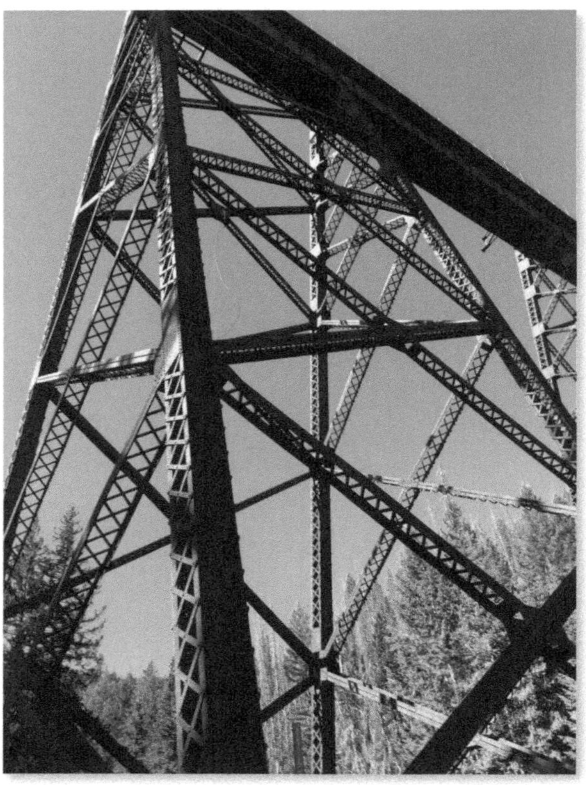

As we're crossing Continental Divide #6, we catch a bike race in progress—the Butte 100—and stop at mile 60 of 100 to cheer on the racers. The Butte 100 is pretty similar to the Leadville 100 in Colorado. Both trails are on extreme single tracks and done on mountain bikes. It's a treat to cheer on other bikers while you're in the midst of a grueling challenge yourself. The race organizers treat us to watermelon and sodas, and we enjoy a casual conversation with them about the progress of our journey and our continued aspiration to finish this trek across the country.

We leave the race and ride into the hills while the temperature continues to climb, until the peak heat of the day at lunch. We are able to find some shade on the back side of a rock, and we enjoy our lunch with a little bit of respite from the heat.

After lunch we pull out the maps and decide to take the alternate route instead of climbing another long, brutal trail over Mt. Fleecer. We end up getting to the turn for Wise River rather early, all things considered, but we still have many miles to go before camping.

Anyway, at the turn for Wise River we stop at a local fishing outfitter, hoping to purchase an ice-cold soda. Unfortunately, he doesn't have any for sale; however, he happily obliges with ice water. We chat for a while about where we're headed, and he confirms that the convenience store ahead is the only place to get food for the next few hundred (!) miles. Once again we realize the benefits of talking with the locals. We thank him for his kindness and directions and get on our way.

The headwind is brutal going up the canyon, and the paved road makes the temperature even hotter, especially when we're making only a four-mile-per-hour pace in the headwind. The Wise River is wide and long, and we can see people swimming, rafting, and fishing. We want nothing more than to trade places with the folks enjoying the river. So, when we see an opening for cars to launch their boats, we stop to at least cool off, even if we don't have the time to go for a swim, given the number of miles still to go before we reach our campsite.

I take off my shoes and socks and sit near the river's edge to cool off my feet and legs. John's odometer is off again, so he's back in the parking lot, bike upside down, spinning his wheel to get the mileage to adjust perfectly with our turn-by-turn directions. I watch a small snake try to figure out how to eat a piece of fish that he had somehow gotten ahold of, but the piece of fish is too big for his mouth. I know the snake will eventually figure out how to eat that fish, but I don't have the time to watch him devour it.

The next stop is the convenience store we learned about when we were chatting with the fishing outfitter. We need to stock up for the next two or three days, so we're going to have to be ready to bear some extra weight. When we get there, the three people we ran into in Helena are also inside stocking up. They had gone up and over Mt. Fleecer, the route we chose to avoid, and they tell us that it was brutally difficult, and in some places not bikeable.

We all head outside and chat while drinking cold Gatorades, eating chips, and condensing the food we just purchased by removing any extra packaging. The less weight you can carry the better, so you learn quickly how to get rid of extra packaging on food before leaving a store.

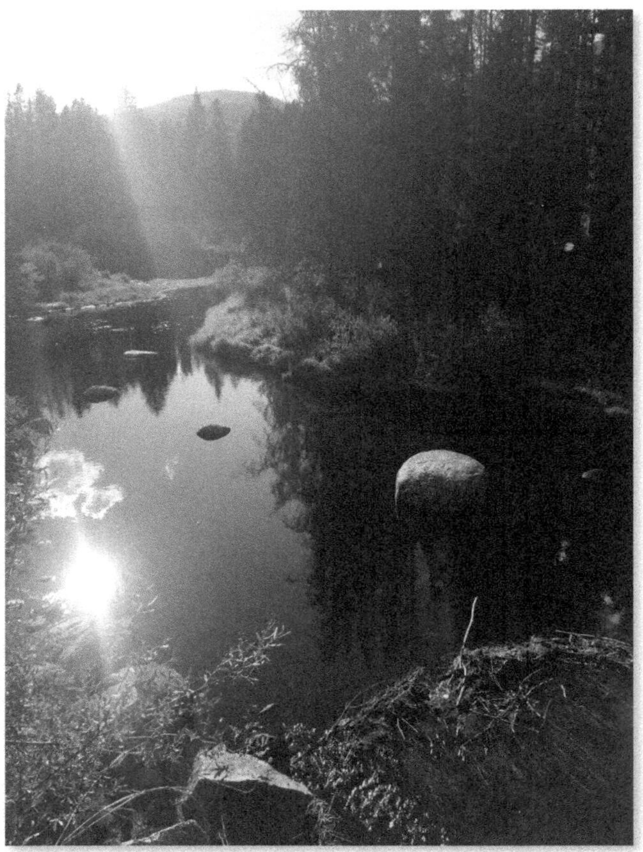

We try to find a hotel before making the Wise River campsite, but there is only one and it's sold out, so we continue on. We pass a small airport, and the windsock is fully inflated, proving that the wind is in our face and that our journey is not going to get any easier during this final leg of the day.

As the sun starts to drop we are treated to a splendid sunset, which creates beautiful refractions of light on the scenery around us. The sun dances off the stream, reflecting the purple, orange, and pink sky like a mirror. The three GDMBR bikers end up stopping frequently to take pictures with their professional-looking cameras. I chose not to bring a heavy camera in order to avoid the extra weight, so it's just the iPhone for me.

Eventually we pull into the Wise River Campgrounds. Our map indicates that there are tons of sites to choose from. The day was long, so I am ready to stop at the first campsite. Camping tonight is devoid of running water, but we are at least on the river, so we are able to restock our water with the drops we have for purification.

I bike up to the first campsite I see with people and ask the family questions about water, showers, etc. I ask if there is water at the next campground, and they eagerly offer us all the water we need. This is trail magic—they supply us with two days' worth of water.

We pitch our tent and get ready for dinner. I go over to their campsite to fill up our water bottles, and to my delight, they offer me their leftover salad. It is a mound of fresh salad, fruit, and—even better—they give me two paper plates to take back to our campsite. After dinner, we hit the river for a bath, and quickly change before heading back to our new friends' campsite as they have invited us for s'mores.

We finish the night around the campfire, cooking the s'mores and enjoying conversation about our lives and journeys. The fire crackles and spits as the marshmallows slowly turn soft, skewered by the sticks we hold over the flames. For the first time since Holland Lake we feel like we have just had family time. We go to bed missing our kids, our dog, and our friends, but we are grateful to have each other on this journey.

Ending day stats:

Start 8:10 a.m. Finish 6:15 p.m.
10 hours and 5 minutes
61.56 miles

GDMBR Day 15
July 31, Sunday

End of week two
Weather—Sun, wind
Wise River Campground to Bannack State Park, MT

John's Notes: The strong headwind yesterday, and the fact that Lima is still 130 miles away, made Bannack State Park the destination for the day. They have running water and a sit-down toilet, so it's all good.

An early start, and a tailwind, make the miles fly.

We wake up early while the other campsites are still asleep. We break down our tent, eat a quick breakfast of Pop-Tarts and hot tea, and head on our way. The climb out of Wise River is long and steep, and at one point I have to stop—choosing a nice field to lie down in and catch my breath. I regroup my brain, thinking about the hot springs on the other side of the mountain, and set back to climbing toward the summit. At least the thick woods are providing shade for the morning climb.

We reach the summit around lunchtime and bike just a few miles down the mountain to where the signs for the hot springs are, and where we'll have lunch.

At lunch, our servers are literally 10 years old. They are helping their folks with the resort, and it is Sunday so many travelers are checking out. After lunch, we take a long soak in the hot springs, and it feels amazing.

A quick break is all we have time for. Even though we had some time for the hot springs, we need to make sure we don't hit the road too late because we don't want to show up late to our next campsite.

Once we descend from the mountain, known as Maverick Mountain Ski Area, the plains of Montana open up in front of us. We leave the dirt roads in the mountains for a sizzling paved freeway. The sun beats down on us. It is hot and dry on the pavement, and the wind makes the ride even drier. Thankfully, the wind is finally with us this time, giving us an extra push.

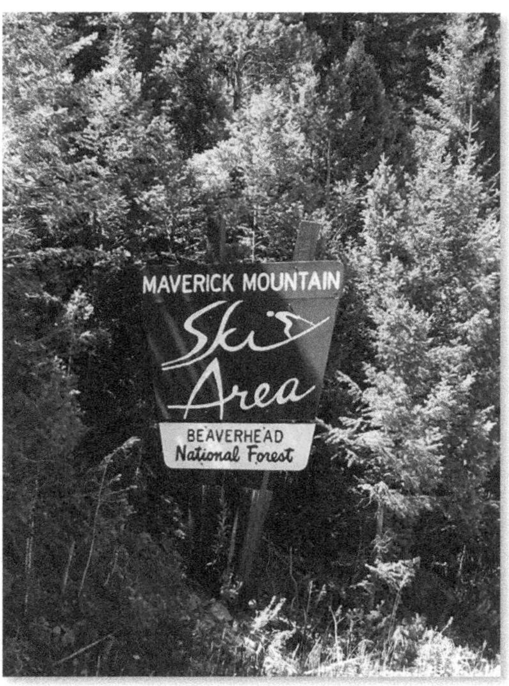

When we reach Bannack State Park we are greeted by the smiles of the three GDMBR bikers from Helena. They are sitting under a shade tree, enjoying a cold soda from the small state park store. In the store, we purchase our camp permit and pitch our tent right next to the camp hosts, who are incredibly nice and friendly. We wash our bodies and our clothes in the river and lay them out to dry in the evening's warm sun.

At the beginning of the trip I remember being worried about what

I would do with the extra time in the woods, and what I would think about. To be honest, just 15 days into this journey, I only want to rest, sleep, and cool off in a river, if I can. I have no thoughts other than fixing dinner, looking at the maps, and reading McCoy's book about the trail so I can get a better idea of what we might encounter on the next day.

This also helps John and me set reasonable distance goals. We try to set goals we will achieve the next day, and the day after that, and all the other days until we reach our final goal of Antelope Wells. This daily goal always dictates what time we have to get up. We have gotten much better at reading the topographical maps, and we now understand how far we can push ourselves.

Today's journey marks the end of section one on the Adventure Cycling Association maps, and we open a new map for the next section of the GDMBR before going to bed. A profound feeling washes over me in the midst of this accomplishment. It is both gratifying and a little surreal. I watch as John resets his cyclometer to sync with the new map and turn-by-turn directions. It is small victories like this that keep us moving day after day on the trail.

We still have five maps and thousands of miles to go, but notching map one to the belt is definitely a start.

Ending day stats:

Start 8:00 a.m. Finish 4:30 p.m.
8 hours and 30 minutes
48.80 miles

GDMBR Day 16
August 1, Monday

Weather—Sun, hot
Bannack State Park to Lima, MT

John's Notes: The elevation chart on the map shows a flat day, which means we can cover some serious distance. Our goal for the day is Lima, an 80-mile ride from Bannack State Park.

It's tough to quench your thirst with hot water.

We get an early start to the day because of the long rest we took yesterday and to beat the heat we know is inevitably going to hit us. The terrain on the trail is turning into desert-like topography, which of course comes with big heat swings. Yet, like the desert, our morning starts cold with frost on the tent. We each put a bunch of layers on to start our ride. This makes for a slow start because it's hard to bike when your movement is restricted by layers. John and I ride out past the cows and greet them with waves and hoots while they moo and snort at us. We leave the cows behind pretty quickly, and the terrain morphs from plains and farms into rocky desert with a winding river close by; you can see the heat shimmer off the trail in front of us and feel the sweat start to drip.

At the midpoint in the day, John and I enjoy a nice downhill stretch on a well-maintained gravel road. Fishermen line the road, casting their flies into the river and waiting for the slightest pull on their rod so they can flick their wrist and set the hook. Campers pull off the road every few miles to stop at the campsites along the river, while John and I keep riding by, determined. We are so in the zone that we eventually pass a deep swimming hole that's clear and bright. It's too late by the time we decide we want a dip, as we're already two miles down the road. We agree it's not worth the energy to turn around.

The day moves on . . .

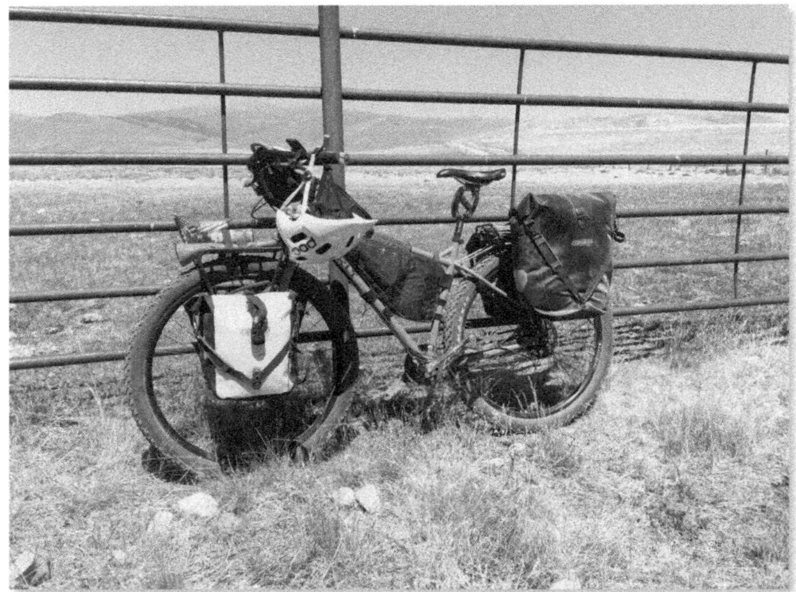

Our route takes us off the gravel road to a paved frontage road in the late afternoon, and the heat kicks up a notch as it reflects off the black pavement below us. There's a headwind to boot, so we move rather slowly in the heat. A little farther on down the road we cross over the Continental Divide Trail (CDT) for hikers, and I am suddenly aware that some people walk this part of the trail, in this heat—thank God we have our bikes!

John and I both feel the long day in a number of ways, mentally as well as physically. We can see the huge signs for Lima on the freeway, and we have only 10 miles left. But we're both starting to struggle, so we stop a few times, which isn't helping us to get there any faster. We are both dehydrated but don't want to drink our now-hot water.

The last hour seems to drag on forever, but we eventually make it. It felt like we were moving in slow motion, which we were. It was definitely a mental struggle.

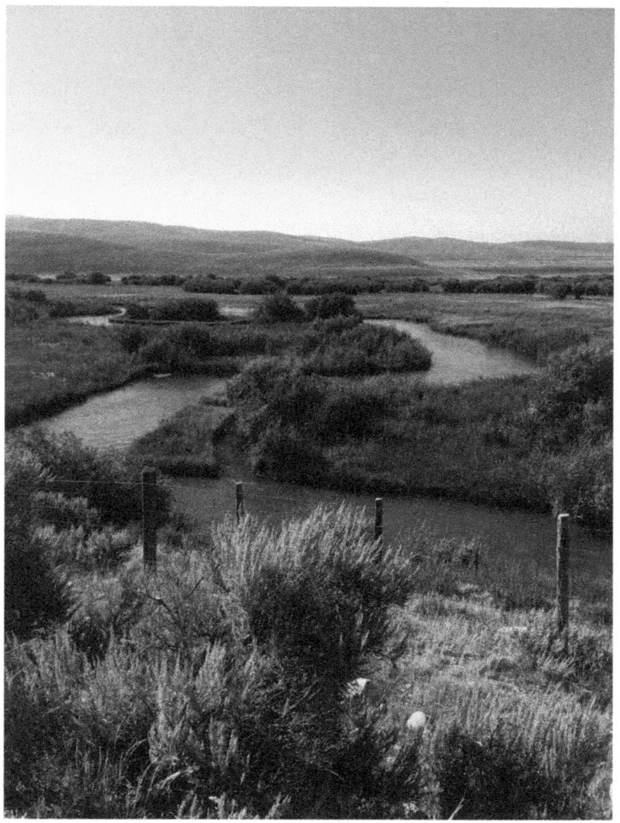

When we get to the Exxon gas station, we each immediately chug a Gatorade before we even get to the counter to pay. It takes a few minutes in the A/C of the gas station store and a couple of cold Gatorades before our heads catch up with our bodies.

Slowly recuperating, John and I notice an old worn chair that's torn in various areas and obviously well-loved, sitting next to the coffee pot. John inquires about the chair, and we learn that it belonged to the gas station owner's father, who used to come to the station every day, drink coffee, nap in the chair, and chat with all the passing customers. The owner hadn't had the desire to move the chair since his father passed away, which was more than a year ago.

Our fathers tend to have a lasting impact on us, no matter the relationship, and we were touched by this man's simple way of remembering his.

Upon leaving the gas station, I become laser-focused on finding a hotel for the night—we don't want to camp after today's long and hot journey. There is only one hotel, and it's our only hope for a bed and a toilet tonight. When we enter the lobby of the hotel, the woman behind the counter takes one look at me and clearly sees my desperation. She tells me that the hotel is full.

However, there are some contractors working on laying IT lines in the town, and one of the contractors may not be arriving until tomorrow. She calls her husband to see if there is any way they can sell the room to us tonight, and he confirms the room is available.

However, when we get to the room we find a pizza in the oven and food all over the countertops of the small kitchen. Someone is obviously using this room. We find out that the contractors who have been here for quite some time are still using the room for a kitchen, even though they aren't paying for it. The woman from the front is not too pleased, and she kicks the contractors out so we can have the room for the night. We feel badly for the contractors, but we are also grateful we have a hotel room with air conditioning for the night.

John and I each take a cold shower and crank the A/C before heading back to the lobby, which actually looks more like a post office. It turns out that many CDT hikers use this hotel as a place to ship their supplies. However, many of the hikers never show up for whatever reason, or cancel, and so the owners of the hotel have a lot of items for others to take, which are displayed in the FREE box. John and I peruse the box for a moment to see if there is anything we need. I take a sharp knife, some almonds, and some small peanut butter packets.

Before we hit the pillow, we get a call from Barney and Krista Stotz, our friends from Florida who offered to support us on part of the route. They are currently at our home in Colorado and packing up to meet us in Yellowstone National Park. John texts them pictures of the map we are using, and we discuss how many days it will take us to get to Flagg Ranch, which is near Yellowstone in Grand Teton National Park. The only things we need to have them bring us are the replacement propane fuel for our small stove and John's new bike seat. John has been suffering with a saddle sore since Banff, and he is hoping that an old-school leather Brooks seat will correct the uncomfortable situation.

Ending day stats:

Start 8:00 a.m. Finish 4:30 p.m.
8 hours and 30 minutes
48.80 miles

GDMBR Day 17
August 2, Tuesday

Weather—Sun, hot
Lima to Lakeview Upper Campground, MT

John's Notes: The heat and wind of yesterday dried us to the bone and it's expected to continue, so the prospect of a swim with a view sounded good. We are due in Flagg Ranch in two days to meet Barney and Krista.

Loving from a dog goes a long way.

We start our morning with some local lovin' from the hotel dog, and can't help thinking of our Nina back home. Our daughter Michelle told us Nina has recuperated nicely—and so far hasn't gotten into any more fights with her host dogs. Breakfast is back at the Exxon gas station with the empty and worn chair next to the coffee pot.

We leave the town behind and start our journey for the day on a compact dirt road next to a winding and curving river. Our wheels move with a steady spin that's quicker than the river next to us. The spokes make the wheels look uniform and precise, whereas the river twists and turns slowly—with a distinct direction. But its path has been sculpted over the course of many years, and it has taken different forms over that time—a beauty in and of itself. Water moving through an arid landscape creates contrasting beauty.

I am jolted from my reverie suddenly as a herd of at least 1,000 head of cattle appear in front of us. We have stumbled upon a cattle drive that is being guided by a 13-year-old cowgirl, Miranda, and her family. Miranda is the picture-perfect cowgirl. Her large brimmed hat helps shade her beautiful face from the scorching sun. Her long-sleeve plaid shirt and long jeans are covered by a light layer of dust. We talk with Miranda about the cattle drive and what life is like as a cowgirl in Montana. Miranda is the only person in her family who speaks English, and she currently attends the local middle school in Lima. She tells us that she and her family had started the cattle drive around 5:00 a.m. that morning, and that they are headed just a few miles down the road.

We take in the sights and sounds of cowboys and cowgirls working the dogs and the cattle, keeping them on their slow trudge forward. We happily enjoy their pace and wait for the herd to reach a point where we can pass. They have offered to clear a section right down the middle of the herd so we can pass through, but John and I have never seen a cattle drive before, and we can see that there is only a mile or so more to go before the cows turn into their new pasture. So we wait with Miranda and her brother.

Eventually we leave the cattle drive behind, and the day continues to warm up until it becomes brutally hot. Shade is a tough commodity to find, and we desperately need some for our lunch stop. Luckily, we come across what seems to be an abandoned cattle stockade around lunchtime and are able to find some shade to hide under.

After lunch, we pass the contractors from the hotel in Lima the day before. They are digging trenches and burying fiber so small towns, like Lima, can have high-speed cable. I develop a respect for these men—sharing the heat with them—thinking about how they leave their families for the summer to dig trenches in the beating sun, and get up day after day to do it again. This is the part of America you rarely see.

Later on we come across a GDMBR biker from Texas who is doing the trail all alone. As we bike down the dusty road together, he tells us his stories from the trail, including an encounter with a bear. He tells us that late one night in his tent he could hear commotion near the dumpster. He grabbed his light and peeked his head out, and there before him stood a grizzly bear, happily foraging. It's odd to think that just popping your head back in and zipping up your tent is the safest course of action. He found it difficult to fall back asleep. When he woke up the next morning the bear was gone. John has seen only one bear on our route—at quite a distance from the trail—so we enjoyed listening to his story, even happier that it wasn't ours. He tells us he is taking his time—enjoying the towns and the people. Personally, I can't imagine prolonging the trip from weeks to months.

Our map shows that there is a welcome center to the campground. Unaware that it closes at 4:00 p.m., we feel lucky to arrive just before that, and we relish every minute of the cool A/C. It is our first time out of the scorching sun all day.

The A/C break becomes even more important when we discover that the campsite is mainly in the sun. Finding shade is difficult, but we are able to find a little bit underneath a tree. We help each other with our chores, from pitching the tent to getting dinner ready. First we unpack our panniers and try to find the best location for the tent. Our friend from Texas and another Divide Rider named Robert are also setting up camp for the night.

John likes to clear all the rocks and debris from the small area our tent lies on. Together we pitch the tent and place all of our sleeping gear inside. We take turns setting up our sleeping bags and sleeping mats. When possible, we wash up and change into our evening attire. I plan the meals and John helps me turn on the small camp stove, so we can have warm soup for dinner or warm tea for breakfast. Tonight we eat the bean and cheese burritos we picked up at the gas station. The burritos had warmed in our panniers during the ride, and they are ready for eating.

There is a lake close by our campsite, so John and I walk down to it and enjoy hanging with the hundreds of flocking birds.

Between the campsite and the lake there is a natural spring of flowing cold, refreshing water that we can drink. One of John's chores is to fill our water at night and, when necessary, add the purification drops. After 17 days on the road we both have our routines, and these routines help us get through each day and prepare for the next day to come.

Ending day stats:

Start 8:45 a.m. Finish 4:45 p.m.
8 hours
57.78 miles

The Trail
Idaho

GDMBR Day 18
August 3, Wednesday

Weather—Sun, hot
Lakeview Upper Campground, MT, to Warm River Camp, ID

John's Notes: Today's goal is to continue south and see what the day brings. After reading about a 30-mile stretch of rail trail built upon volcanic ash, our goal is to reach Warm River Campground.

We hope the river is warm . . .

Our morning begins before the sun takes its rise and dawn slowly fades from a dark and motionless sky to a horizon dominated by the red glow of the sun shrouded in a veil by the forest fires in Idaho close by—there is stunning beauty in the smoky sky. Although the smoke creates a majestic sunrise, we're worried about the fire and what the day might bring. We are able to depart earlier than usual. Robert has already packed up and left while the Texan is sound asleep. The map shows that we will be going through some small towns. We were both looking forward to stopping at a restaurant for lunch.

We are finally in "the zone" of the GDMBR; eat, ride, sleep. It took 18 days to get to this mindset! For me, my transition from work life to trail life has finally materialized. Regardless how much I love my work, there is something beyond work! And today I found it.

Shortly after leaving camp, we are faced with a climb to the top of one of the many Continental Divide crossings. John and I are pleasantly surprised with our ability to climb the hill so easily.

Once we get to the summit, we notice the peculiarity of a carving in the Red Rock Pass elevation sign. It shows the silhouette of a man with moose antlers growing out of his head, carrying a heavy load and holding an axe. What does it mean?

Soon after summiting the Continental Divide we see smoke from the fire on the horizon, and we begin to get anxious about what lies ahead. However, as we're descending the hill, the topography changes dramatically, and the smoke disappears as we drop in elevation. Our further progress down the trail brings us to trees and shade, a welcome respite from the sun we have endured over the past few days.

Most mornings, we stop between 9:00 and 10:00 to enjoy a snack and walk our bikes for a few minutes. After two or three hours in the saddle, a short break from pedaling is what the body and mind need. Today we find a tree that appears dead, yet upon closer inspection is definitely alive. Based on the size, it's clearly very old!

As we descend, our route takes us off the main road and into some thick woods. The driver of a red jeep honks at me not too long after John and I enter the woods. The jeep pulls up next to me, and we chat for a bit. Turns out the one behind the wheel, a 12-year-old, is learning to drive. They've stopped to warn me about the bears in the area, and because John has ridden ahead of me and is no longer visible, they are concerned for my safety.

The father in the front seat tells me to make a ton of noise. I tell him that the bear bell on my bike is broken, so he turns around to check the back seat to see if he has an extra one. As he turns to look, I catch a glimpse of his shirt, a skydiving shirt. I ask about it, and he tells me he owns a jump school in New Jersey. So does a friend of ours, and it turns out this guy knows Billy Richards, who owns The Ranch, a jump school in New York. It's moments like this that remind you how small the world is.

John cycles back to me, to check on my safety, and meets the guys in the car. I take a quick video of them and send a fun message to Billy. Then we say our goodbyes, as we need to get back on the trail to get to our next spot.

Shortly after leaving the woods in Idaho, we reach the small town on our map and look for a good lunch spot. We see Robert at the local coffee shop, but we don't stop as we want real food. I can't tell you how excited I am to order fresh food. After lunch, we replenish our food supply at the local gas station, because our stop for the night is going to be another campground. The restaurant allows us to fill our water containers with ice so that we can have cold water on our way to the campground.

And of course, with each passing day, there is always a new challenge. Today is no different. Almost immediately after leaving the gas station, we are met with our next challenge of the day: 31 miles of old railroad bed left behind by the Union Pacific Railroad, which gave railroad access to Yellowstone National Park starting in 1907. The rails have been removed, and all that remain are 31 miles of soft sand and volcanic ash. This is like biking from Ft. Lauderdale to Miami—on the sand! The heat is just as bad. Thank God for the captivating sights along the way, like the railroad bridge, the river with the most beautiful water I have ever seen, and the mature trees.

John and I talk about all the people who must have built this 31-mile stretch of track for the railway, and the lives they must have lived. Both sides of the path are lined by trees, so we are able to get some heat relief while our legs keep spinning through the sand—we aren't moving more than six miles per hour. Just as we're about to finish the final part of the sandy trail, I bury my front tire. Coming to a complete stop, I take the first fall off my bike. I even rip my pants!

We steadily get closer to our destination, and the closer we get, the more we go downhill, all the while feeling a cool breeze rising up from the river close by. (The breeze is even more noticeable with the rip in my pants!) The river is wide, with many boulders making it look picture perfect. The trail is right on the cliff of the river, which is down below. The sounds from the river are constant and loud—very soothing.

When we finally make it to our campsite, we're treated to one of our better camping experiences on the trail: the Warm River Campground. It turns out to be just as pristine and picturesque as the Adventure Cycling Association describes. Kids, dogs, and families are all playing in the river and enjoying the cool water.

We bike over to the campsite host where we need to pay our fee. I notice he's drinking red wine, so I ask him where I can buy some. He tells me, "Sixteen miles away in Ashton." He must have taken pity on me, as all I have is a bicycle. He kindly sells me a bottle of red wine, corks it for me, and sends his wife over to our campsite with some wood for the night.

After setting up camp, we can't wait to wash off in the river and clean the caked lava dirt from our bodies. When John takes off his socks, we see a clear sock line between his clean feet and his dirty ash-gray legs. Robert, the Divide Rider from Canada, pulls into the campsite a few minutes after we do and sets up camp right next to us. We share our stories and struggles of the day and talk about the beauty of the trail. Before we realize it, night is already upon us, and John and I set to planning the next day's goal.

The sun takes its bow.

Ending day stats:
Start 7:53 a.m. Finish 6:15 p.m.
10 hours and 25 minutes
65.98 miles

The Trail
Wyoming

GDMBR Day 19
August 4, Thursday

Weather—Sun
Warm River Camp, ID, to Flagg Ranch, WY

John's Notes: Although the industrial-strength camping scene of Flagg Ranch does not sound very appealing, it is the easiest place for us to rendezvous with our friends Barney and Krista.

The wheat fields in Idaho are a pleasant surprise.

Leaving Warm River Campground in the morning is bittersweet. John and I love being outdoors and participating in all the recreation available, and we don't have enough time to enjoy a float on the river or take a leisurely day. We add this spot to our list of places we want to come back to.

The morning's climb from the riverbed takes us from rugged trees and rivers to flat plains of the most beautiful fields of golden wheat! Shortly thereafter, we see a sign for the Squirrel Creek Cabins and Cafe for breakfast. The owner informs us we just missed Richard. We chow down on some pancakes, ordering enough to fuel our bodies for the upcoming climbs.

We are now approaching the Wyoming border. The cyclometer keeps saying we are only nine miles away, but it feels like we're not getting any closer. There isn't a cloud in the sky, and the sun beats down on us relentlessly. The dirt road is rough with a lot of loose rocks. About every 10 minutes or so John and I get covered in a blanket of dirt by a passing car or truck. It is not making this stretch any easier. When we reach the sign for the Wyoming state line—shot through with multiple bullets of various sizes—I stop to take a picture. Canada, Montana, and Idaho are behind us!

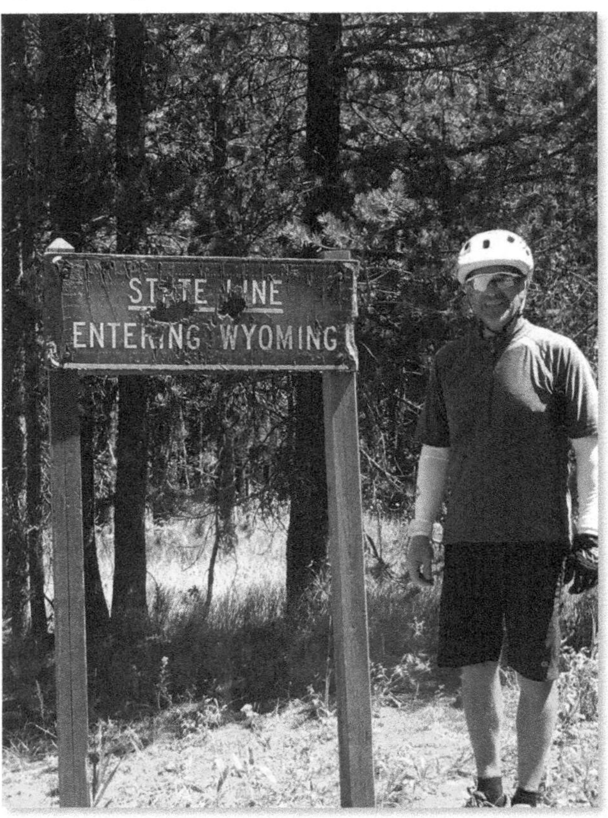

I am immediately struck by vast beauty when we enter the John D. Rockefeller section of the national forest shortly after entering Wyoming. The trees come alive, and the wind rustles through the thick and abundant branches. Then all of a sudden, we're biking through the charred ruins of a forest fire—and the area charred is massive. I am not sure how long ago the fire was, but I am so sad I can't even stop to take a photo.

Eventually, we reach the Flagg Ranch Campsite near Yellowstone National Park. As John said, it is an industrial-size campsite. There are RVs and buses everywhere. This is not the type of camping we've been experiencing so far on the trail. When we get to the huge parking lot at Flagg Ranch, we notice our pickup truck. Immediately we are beyond excited because inside the truck are our friends. After a long embrace with them, we head to the main office to see if we can get a campsite for the night. All campsites are completely sold out.

Regardless of the availability of campsites, I have to shower. We have been in the woods for a few days—I stink! I need to brush my teeth, wash my hair, and just get out of the clothing I have been biking in for the past several days. So John and I park the bikes and start a load of laundry while I enjoy a long hot shower. While I am in the shower, John runs into Robert and helps him find someone to share a campsite with. John and I can worry about our campsite later with Barney and Krista.

We intentionally chose to do this portion of the ride with Barney and Krista. We are so glad to have some of our friends for company. Not to mention the fact that they came with a truckful of luxuries we can't get on the trail.

A sit-down dinner experience is available at the park, and I need more time to finish my laundry. Then we enjoy a nice hot meal with Barney and Krista. Robert shows up at the restaurant with his new camping friend. He has his maps out, and we can see him explaining the route to his dinner partner.

After dinner, we need to find a place to camp. Barney thinks he spotted a place to possibly camp on the way in to meet us, so we follow the truck a couple miles away from Flagg Ranch, and come up to a "campsite" that is actually a hunting site where hunters can hang their deer on a post and lintel to drain the blood. Of course, the risk of bears comes to mind, but there is nowhere else to camp, and the last light of day is leaving the hills. So we take the risk and pitch a tent. At least there is an outhouse fairly close by.

Ending day stats:

Start 8:50 a.m. Finish 5:15 p.m.
8 hours and 25 minutes
49.83 miles

GDMBR Day 20
August 5, Friday

Weather—Sun, cold, overcast
Flagg Ranch to Lava Motel, WY

John's Notes: Our intent is to bike a short 47-mile day—taking in the beauty of Jackson Lake and the Tetons. We plan a stop at the pizzeria at Leeks Marina on Jackson Lake. Concluding the day at Togwotee Mountain Lodge is our goal.

There is a point where you finally feel like you are in shape. After 20 days on the trail, we feel that way.

We wake up early with frost on the inside of our tent. Camping by the river brings dew to our tent, and it covers our bikes in white frost. This is the coldest morning yet. Because of the weather, Barney and Krista's first day with us starts out as an adventure.

Having them along is already bringing benefits, as we are able to enjoy hot coffee and fresh fruit with breakfast—while sitting in chairs. Small comforts we no longer take for granted! We are able to choose from an abundance of food to take with us in our panniers for the day's journey—all huge luxuries when on the GDMBR.

After packing up our equipment, John and I start our climb out of the valley—while Barney and Krista finish packing their gear. We are quickly struck by the power and grandeur of the Grand Tetons all around us. It's easy to see why so many people come to visit this place of extraordinary beauty. Being on a bike allows us to stop anytime and anywhere to take photos. This is a blessing in the midst of the Tetons, and I grab some great shots.

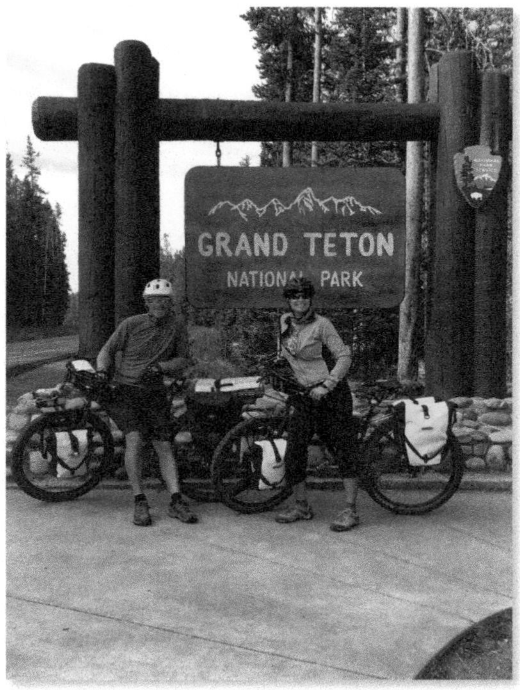

We bike to our first summit fairly quickly, and the next 25 miles are paved and mostly downhill, which gives us time to rest up for the hills of the afternoon. We take the recommended two-mile detour to Leeks Pizza. Because it's mostly downhill to the pizza place, we arrive nearly two hours before it opens. However, we just don't have the patience to hang out; I do love pizza, but today I'm not willing to wait.

Farther down the route we bike to a small cafe, and shortly thereafter, Robert arrives. John and I order enough food for a small army—two salads, two grilled-cheeses, a peanut-butter-and-jelly, and we both order homemade pie. Robert orders coffee and ice cream. And we wonder, how is he going to keep on biking with so little fuel?

The summer wildfires are apparent, and smoke casts a haze on the Tetons. Today there are 20 wildfires burning in Wyoming alone, and drinking water becomes more of a necessity because of the dry, hot smoky air. Early in the afternoon we easily reach our planned goal of Togwotee Mountain Lodge. Having Barney and Krista along adds one more element of planning. When we get to the gas station we leave a note for them, as our cell service doesn't work. We inform them that we feel great and plan to keep going. The gas station attendant knows the route and the area. He informs us there is a motel just 24 miles over the Divide. As we pull out of the gas station we see our trusty gold pickup truck and we get to tell Barney and Krista our new plans.

We reach our crossing #8 of the Continental Divide, and from the summit we clearly see the smoke's origin. The mountains on our route are on fire, and we can see the orange flames. The route takes us to the left, and we find ourselves in the most beautiful rugged shale mountain peaks, but the trail is in the thick of the woods. Once again, Barney and Krista come on our trail from the opposite side. I ask them how far it is to the next lodge, and Barney says, "Not far." Meanwhile, Krista is shaking her head in disagreement. So John and I put our heads down, determined to get to the motel and happy that we didn't just bike the freeway (the shortest route) to the second lodge, down the road.

At the Lava mountain lodge the four of us head to the bar to watch the opening ceremonies of the 2016 summer Olympics in Rio. We share a large gourmet vegetarian pizza and homemade brownie sundae prepared by the lodge's world-class chef. The four of us talk about our different experiences over the course of the day. Barney is shocked at how truly hard the route is, telling us that you don't really know how hard it is until you drive it.

They described their day. In the morning, they took their time packing up camp. Then they drove to Yellowstone—but found it too crowded, so they decided to just enjoy the beautiful vistas and scenery around them. They stopped at Jackson Lake for a picnic and to take pictures. Barney had brought his good camera, and they took several photos of us biking together. They were curious to see how far we had gotten, so they studied the route map and realized it would be easier for them to stick to the paved roads. They caught up with us at Togwotee Mountain Lodge gas station and drove on ahead to get our hotel room.

Tonight, after the sunset, we take in the cool night air on the back deck of the lodge and stare out at burning hills blotched with the bright red of burning embers on fallen trees and brush. We start to worry about our route for tomorrow, and after doing some research we discover that both the main route and alternate route are closed. There is the possibility of the alternate route opening in the next day or two.

We decide to hit the hay and hope it opens tomorrow, as our only other option is to bike back to Yellowstone and go through Jackson Hole, adding a couple of extra days to our trip and an extra 150 miles of paved highway biking.

Ending day stats:

Start 8:20 a.m. Finish 7:15 p.m.
10 hours and 55 minutes
71.22 miles

GDMBR Day 21
August 6, Saturday

Weather—Sun, overcast, rain, fire
Lava Mountain Lodge to Whiskey Grove, WY

John's Notes: Even though we had gone farther yesterday than we'd intended, and the miles were tough and long, we woke up feeling ready for the day. We knew with the visible forest fires from the motel that it could pose new challenges. The map showed a four-mile climb through the fire zone. Then there was the climb of Union Pass at 9,210 feet, making Whiskey Grove Campground another long day.

When people go out of their way for you—take notice.

In the morning we call the fire headquarters to see if our route is open, and we are disappointed to hear that our route is directly in the middle of one of the major fires. We ask about the alternate route and are encouraged to hear that it is currently open. We are good to go.

John and I head down the valley, and Barney bikes with us for the first part of the journey. There are posted fire signs showing us directly where the fire is and how dangerous the air quality is. It is highly recommend that we stay indoors and not go outside. Local children have made thank you signs for the firemen and posted them all over the fences of the area they are working in.

Barney gets picked up by Krista after we start to climb. They have a full day of exploring planned, as we are in such a beautiful area. At one of the last switchbacks on the hill, we cross paths with a US Forest Service officer who stops us and tells us that the road is closed and we will have to turn around. He instructs us to go downhill and wait it out for a couple of hours while he goes and checks on the status of the route. We begrudgingly head downhill, a five-mile hill we have just spent an hour climbing. Turning around to descend a big hill that you have just climbed is a challenge mentally.

After a couple hours of waiting, the officer returns and tells us that he was given permission from his superiors to allow us back on the route and through the pass. The officer told us he checked on our story about calling, and confirmed that the woman on the phone had indeed told us the road was open. She did not realize we weren't locals, as the road was open for them only. So here we are, in the middle of a huge forest fire, and the officer takes time out of his day to truly help us.

This is the spirit of the trail.

He informs us we can pass through the fire zone as long as we promise to continue and not stop. We show him our map and exactly where we're headed—which happens to be away from the fire. John then asks if he could give us a lift to the top of the hill, since we already biked it once, and he graciously agrees.

We pile our bikes into the back of his truck; I get to sit in the cab, while John is in the back. I ask about the fires, and he shares that we have come at the end of the three-week fire, a new crew is on their way in, and that they would all be going home tomorrow. They were able to save all the homes, with only one back patio burnt pretty badly.

We will never forget the kindness of this officer, and we are forever grateful for what he did for us.

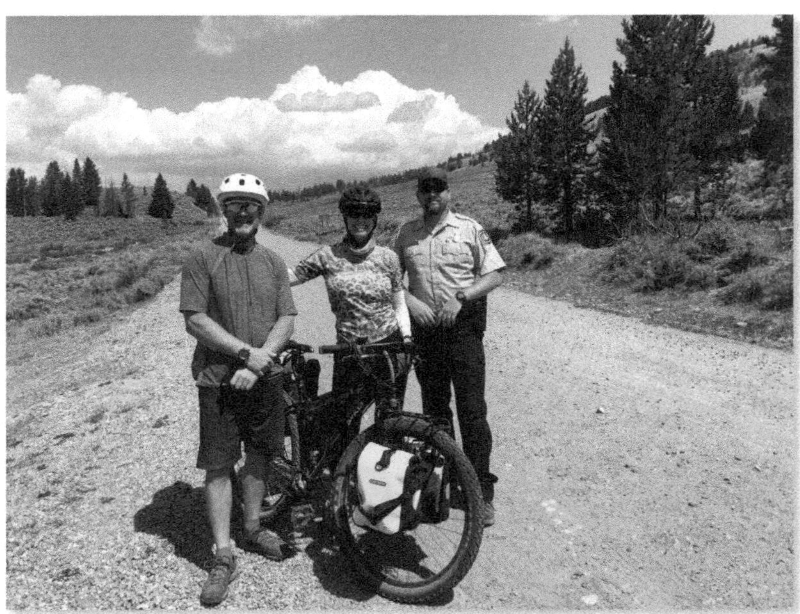

As we leave the officer, the armed guard, and the road blockades behind, we find that the fire road is steep and rocky. The sun is hot, but the clouds have started to form, and you can tell that rain is going to give the firemen some relief very soon.

We crest the summit at Continental Divide crossing #9, and are able to find a bit of shade in the shadow cast from the US Forest sign at the top of the Divide. To our tremendous surprise, we spot a gold truck in the distance—Barney and Krista. Barney received special approval to drive through the danger area in support of us. He said he sweet-talked the firemen and told them he would be personally responsible for our safety.

We never see or feel the heat from the fire, but the smell is evident and strong, and the quality of air is noticeably different. Of course, we know that where there is smoke, there is usually fire, so we descend from the summit quickly in order to ensure we don't put ourselves in harm's way.

The fire delay has set us back today, and after lunch it is already 2:00 p.m. We still have 38 miles to go with varying elevation changes in the topography ahead. Going down the trail, the rocky washboard road is brutal on our bodies as our bikes don't have dual shocks. We have to use our brakes often on the downhill to avoid bouncing our panniers off our bikes.

At 5:00 p.m. we are still 17 miles from the campground, and the road continues to get rougher. Every muscle in my body now aches. We keep moving forward—silent and determined. I break the silence eventually to ask John if he is having fun. Struck by the silliness of my query, I burst out laughing, because this is not fun. Hard work is not fun, but the feeling of accomplishment is.

Upon cycling into Whiskey Grove Campground, we see our friends have been setting up camp, and it is perfect. The river is flowing in the background, Barney has the campfire burning, and Krista has a hot meal prepared and the picnic table set. They even manage to find my favorite bottle of wine, Rombauer Zin. We quickly take a bath in the ice-cold river and then pitch our tent so we can join our friends for the evening.

It's times like this when we are overwhelmed with gratitude. We can't help but reflect on how much we take for granted on a daily basis. Life is about the journey, and about realizing when special moments in your life happen.

I remind myself to make sure I acknowledge and celebrate the small things that make life grand. Today was grand in so many ways.

Ending day stats:
Start 8:20 a.m. Finish 6:15 p.m.
9 hours and 55 minutes
58.38 miles

GDMBR Day 22
August 7, Sunday

End of week three
Weather—Light rain to heavy rain
Whiskey Grove to Little Sandy Creek, WY

John's Notes: Today's ride from Whiskey Grove Campground to Little Sandy Creek Campground will be 84.9 miles—the entire route is mostly flat and 60 miles are paved. Pinedale will come at mile 35 and offer a full-service grocery and hot lunch options.

Some days it's best to take one step back
to take two steps forward.

We wake up to the beautiful sound of the flowing river. The chill in the air is refreshing, and a soft, light rain is dropping. Barney gets the campfire going while Krista starts hot water for coffee, tea, and pancakes. John and I work on breaking down our tent and packing our equipment. Within an hour of awakening, after a quick breakfast, we are on the road. The first stop on our route is the small town of Pinedale. We're totally appreciating paved road all the way after the washboard terrain at the end of yesterday.

Barney joins us on his mountain bike close to town, and the three of us arrive together. As we enter town, there are a huge moose and her baby eating leaves from a tree in the local park. I have never seen a moose this close before, and we stop to take in her beauty. As a large truck noisily passes the moose, she turns her body to protect her baby. You could immediately see how she could easily kill something trying to get to her calf.

Lunch is at an authentic Mexican restaurant, and totally delicious. After restocking at the grocery store on the way out of town, we put our heads down and set our minds to reaching the goal of Little Sandy Creek Campground, Wyoming. As we ride the flat paved roads, we get closer to the small town of Boulder, which is also the turn on the route. We feel excited and apprehensive about the darkness of the clouds, the frequency of the lightning, and the intensity of the thunder, which is growing closer, but the rain is light, so we press on. By the time we make it to the convenience store in Boulder, the storm intensifies, the sky lights up with the crack of thunder, and just seconds later the storm hits us from directly overhead. It starts raining sideways, and we have to hide inside the store to avoid getting totally drenched. Then the electricity in the gas station suddenly sputters and dies.

Barney and Krista had driven ahead to scope out the campsite before the rain hit. After noticing how strong the storm was, they head back to find us, where we're sheltered in the dark gas station. Turns out, the rain is not going to stop for quite some time, so we have two options: 1) Bike through the rain and camp in the campsite we are headed toward, nearly 40 miles away; or 2) go back to Pinedale and find a hotel.

We choose option #2, and it turns out to be a GREAT decision for three reasons: We are able to enjoy the amenities a hotel room offers;

we snag an awesome dinner at a local brewery; and finally, after the rain stops, our day ends with a stunning sunset.

Ending day stats:
Start 8:00 a.m. Finish 2:20 p.m.
6 hours and 20 minutes
47.6 miles

GDMBR Day 23
August 8, Monday

Weather—Sun, cool to hot, favorable tailwind
Boulder to Atlantic City, WY

John's Notes: The small setback for a half day of riding makes us think that we can push farther, as our home in Clark, Colorado, is only a few days away. We miss our family, our friends, and our dog terribly, and agree to push hard to make it home for the weekend.

We can smell the barn . . . (Colorado is just a few days away).

With rested legs and a great attitude we are able to get our earliest start of the trip. The day starts with breakfast at the hotel, and by 7:00 a.m. we are packed up. Barney drives us back to Boulder, where we had our journey cut short yesterday. It's only 42 degrees when we start, but at least the sun is out.

We cross the Continental Divide for the 10th time early in the morning, and keep at our torrid pace as today's goal of Atlantic City will be quite the physical test. We have read about how the Wyoming winds blow the entire time and the dry roads quickly turn to dust. The route takes us along the top of the Divide, allowing us to see for miles and make our 11th crossing. We are a long way from anything, with many more miles to go. This is exactly the scenic view I know John was looking forward to on this trip.

The desert-like topography is quite beautiful—vast, wide open, nothing but nature. There are a few cows that we see occasionally or some antelope. The white puffy clouds above are nice contrasts to the blue sky. There are no telephone lines, no houses, no real feel of humans at all, with the exception of the long roads that are lightly traveled by a few bikers and cars.

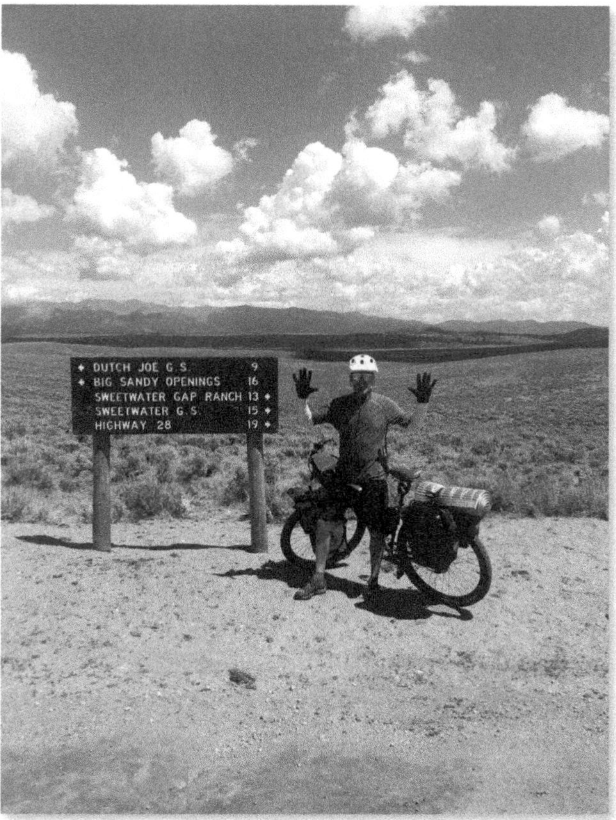

Toward the end of the afternoon the inside of my leg starts to cramp and hurt. My legs are tired again from overuse, and today's long trek is beginning to take its toll. We stop in the historic South Pass City, and then press onward through another steep hill to climb. Just when we think we can't make it any farther, we finally hit downhill into Atlantic City.

Near the bottom of the hill, we see Barney's familiar face on his mountain bike and appreciate his cheering us on. Tonight we will not be camping as Barney and Krista were able to find a cabin to rent. The owners, Mike and Patricia, are big supporters of GDMBR riders. We are greeted warmly by all of them. Patricia learns of my aching leg and brings some Epsom salt, magnesium pills, and homemade chamomile tea to our cabin.

They share racers' stories with us and tell us all about their sustainable cabin, built to stay off the grid. The bathtub has hot water from solar energy, the lights are LED, and the chamomile was harvested in the front yard. They share with us how lucky we are to get the one night they had open, as the cabin is booked solid for the next two weeks.

We enjoy another amazing meal, cooked by Krista, of salmon, potatoes, and steamed veggies. We plan for tomorrow's journey and then go to sleep in a soft and warm bed. Barney and Krista head off into the small historic mining town for some adventure, where they find that the bar is still open and has a large selection of historical tools, small machinery, and friendly locals.

Ending day stats:

Start 7:35 a.m. Finish 6:15 p.m.
10 hours and 40 minutes
74.77 miles

GDMBR Day 24
August 9, Tuesday

Weather—Sun, wind
Atlantic City to A&M Reservoir campsite, WY
Great Basin Crossing

John's Notes: Even with yesterday's long day, we have great determination to get home to Colorado for the weekend. Our plan is to reach A&M Reservoir, through nearly 80 miles of barren, dusty, and windy trail. The Great Basin, with its wind and lack of water, has a daunting reputation among GDMBR riders. Today's section is the number one reason we asked Barney and Krista to join us. We had read how incredibly hard this section would be.

Two flat tires and a touch of luck.

We set the alarm for 5:30 a.m. We know that the Great Basin crossing is going to be long, hot, and challenging, as the Great Basin is the largest area of contiguous endorheic watersheds in North America. If there is a section on the map where we would need or want support, this is it; in order to make our goal, we have to get an early start.

It's a very cold start, and my leg is already sore right from the beginning. It feels like a bruise, not like a pulled muscle; yet it's probably the latter, and it's definitely slowing me down. John and I put our heads down and ride for three hours on the long and flat dirt road before saying a word. Then, we are suddenly pulled from our intense focus by the sound of thundering hooves galloping next to us—wild horses! John has often talked about the wild horses in Wyoming. The wild horse herds of Wyoming are an integral part of our shared history, and their beauty should be protected. Seeing them in person is truly breathtaking.

There are a few black cows out here, but it doesn't seem as if there is much to eat or drink. A wild black horse is hanging out with the black cows, and I wonder if they think they are cousins or something.

We have not seen a car or truck for hours. It's getting close to 12:30, and Barney and Krista should be along soon for lunch. This is the section of the route where we really need them. There is no water, food, or shade. The wind is in our faces and mental determination is the only thing keeping us going. Seconds before we head down a long hill we hear Barney honking; we look back and see him jump out of the car, frantically waving his hands. Why isn't he driving the short distance to us? This seems really odd. Well, we soon find out; with two flat tires, it is a wonder they were able to make it this far.

The rocks on the route have punctured the sidewall on one tire and are about to destroy the second tire. Barney and John change the first tire while Krista and I make lunch. The wind is howling, and we use the truck for wind protection. We've got 40 miles to go and the wind is only getting stronger. My leg is hurting significantly, so I take some pretty strong pain pills, remainders from my recent back surgery, in order to make it through the day.

After lunch, John and I move on while Barney and Krista take the car back a few miles to an oil-pump house, desperately in search of a patch or plug for the second tire. There are no services, businesses, or people for hundreds of miles, so the oil-drilling maintenance facility, just miles back, is their only option. When they arrive, there happens to be an employee on duty, and Barney and Krista are able to sweet-talk him into helping them out. They find a plug for the tire and are able to repair it. Since they had two flat tires, the spare would have to work as the second repair.

Shortly after lunch, on the trail, we see a bike fully loaded for touring, with no rider. As we bike closer, we notice a human resting under an abandoned tractor. The wind is so strong, it just pushes us around.

We meet the fellow, who had decided to take a rest under the shade of the tractor to see if the wind would calm down. His goal for the night is Atlantic City, and we tell him what a great town it is.

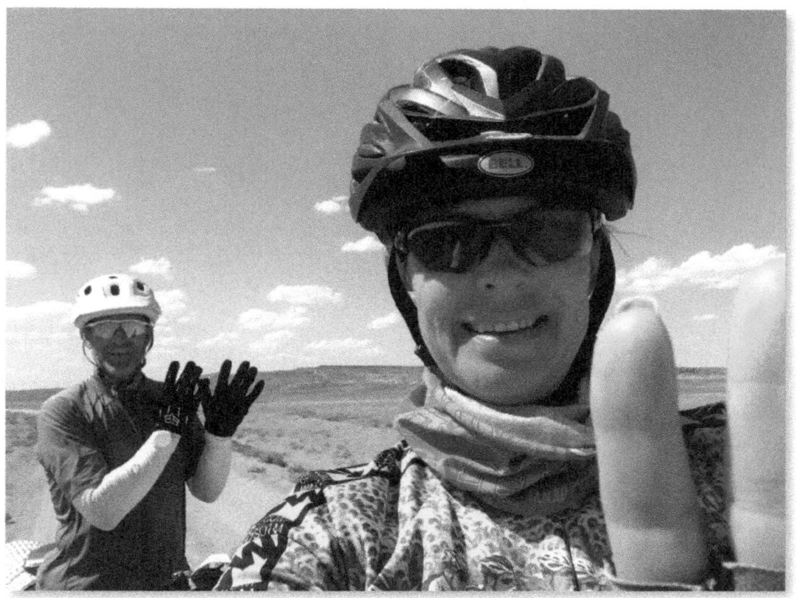

A number of miles later, we cross the Continental Divide for the 13th time. This gives us a boost in motivation to keep moving forward. On one of our final turns, there is a 30-mile-per-hour headwind, and according to the map, a seven-mile climb. I draft behind John, but with the wind, we can only bike at three miles per hour. This is slower than you can walk when you're in a hurry. My leg aches so badly that I want to stop and cry, but I am determined to keep moving. Besides, where will I go? We are crossing the Great Basin. This section is hard. There is no quitting.

At the last turn of the day the wind comes to our aid instead of our detriment. My leg twinges with pain every time I push my pedal, but John is incredibly supportive and I pray to God to help me find the strength to continue. Barney joins us on his mountain bike for the final mile of the ride and encourages me to finish the day. At 7:22 p.m.—over 12 hours after leaving the comfy bed in Atlantic City—we reach camp.

To think that the GDMBR racers average 184 miles a day is superhuman. We are totally and completely exhausted after just 79 miles.

When we get to A&M Reservoir, the beauty of the pristine pond and its surroundings is very calming. I am barely able to get off my bike and take off my clothes. I head for the pond to soak. John pitches the tent by himself, and he is able to do so rather easily now that the wind has finally calmed down. Krista has dinner and some good wine waiting after I get out of the pond, and Barney has an inviting campfire started. When we reflect upon this hard and difficult day, John talks about those who traveled the Oregon Trail long before us and made it through the Great Basin. He said, "I felt their spirit surround us as we crossed the Great Basin."

Ending day stats:

Start 7:05 a.m. Finish 7:22 p.m.
12 hours and 17 minutes
79.4 miles

GDMBR Day 25
August 10, Wednesday

Weather—Sun, wind
A&M Reservoir to Rawlins, WY

John's Notes: Our goal today is short, as we are only trying to get to Rawlins, Wyoming, where full services can be found. To beat the heat and the wind, we must get an extra-early start.

Today is a mind-over-pain thing.

We had pushed hard across the Great Basin, and our bodies are feeling the long miles and time in the saddle. My right hamstring hurts bad—like a knife is stabbing through my leg on every pedal stroke. I don't know if I can continue the journey, but home is just three days away, so I continue on. We hope a shorter day to Rawlins will give me some rest and still keep us on a good pace to reach our ranch by Friday.

The sunrise for breakfast is spiritual. The clouds give color and depth to the orange-and-yellow sun reflecting on the pond. It's cold enough in the morning for a campfire, and Barney gets one started. The coyotes howl in the early morning chill. The cows are on the back side of the reservoir having a morning drink.

By 6:45 a.m. we are on our way to Rawlins, Wyoming. From Rawlins, it is about 100 miles to our ranch in Clark, Colorado. Before lunch, we cross the Divide for the 14th time. The road turns from dirt to pavement, and we are able to bike a rather easy ride. When we reach the hotel, I ice my leg and totally chill (no pun intended) for the afternoon. Even though it's a 56-mile day, stopping early always feels like cheating. It just feels weird not to bike until six or seven at night. Still, my body needs the rest.

Anyway, the stop gives us time to enjoy our final day with Barney and Krista. The truck tires check out, so there is nothing more to do until we get back to Steamboat. After seven amazing days with their support, it is time to say goodbye. It's bittersweet because we enjoy their company and the small luxuries they afford us. Soon we'll be joined by another friend, Mark, from Florida. Barney and Krista are heading back to Steamboat Springs in the morning to pick up Mark and drop him off at the Colorado and Wyoming border so he can join us for the epic ride across Colorado.

Ending day stats:

Start 6:45 a.m. Finish 1:15 p.m.
6 hours and 30 minutes
55.96 miles

GDMBR Day 26
August 11, Thursday

Weather—Rain, sun, wind
Rawlins to a primitive campsite (near Aspen Alley), WY

John's Notes: With the prospect of being in Colorado the next morning, with the shade of an aspen tree available to us after almost a week of not seeing one tree, the romantic vision of Aspen Alley drew us on. The potential for high winds still raises the prospect for another hard day.

The support of good friends, on a long journey, lifts the spirits.

We are up extra early today because, for the first time in five days, our map shows elevation ahead of us—hills! We leave the comfort of the hotel and head to the trail. The rainy morning blesses us with a rainbow to start the day. Familiar smells, sights, and sounds make up our journey. As we get closer to our ranch, everything is starting to look and feel more familiar, more like Colorado.

With the rest I got yesterday, my leg is less painful. I am determined to finish this ride with John, no matter what it takes. The Great Basin felt like sea-level compared to the rugged mountains we are now climbing as we head toward Colorado. One of the hills we climb is lined with wild mums (flowers). It's amazing to see how many mums there are living and thriving on the side of a dry dirt road. At the top of the hill, we cross the

Continental Divide for the 15th time and celebrate 1500 miles biked. We are past the halfway point! It's hard to believe we have only 1275 miles left for the entire trip.

In the late afternoon, the sky turns from sunny back to gray and rain, so we put on our rain gear and keep riding. Within an hour the rain stops and we are able to put our rain gear back in our packs. It's better to just get wet and dry out on the bike, if we can, once the rain stops. I use my rain pants more for warmth at night than I do on the route for rain.

Reaching Aspen Alley is a big treat. It's well known on the route because the entire road, on both sides, is lined with tall aspen trees. Once we reach our final spot of the day, we spend the next four miles looking for a place to camp. John scouts out a few primitive campsite potentials while I rest on the side of the road. There is a site by the stream, but it's next to a huge herd of free-range sheep, so we move on.

Then John finds a site that's perfect. It's close to the stream, making it easy to refill and treat our water. As we cross into Colorado, we are leaving the prospects of grizzly bears behind. John hangs our food for, we hope, the last time. It's too windy for a campfire, so we pitch our tent, eat our dinner, and go to bed.

The hardest miles are the ones after you thought you were done for the day.

Ending day stats:
Start 7:10 a.m. Finish 5:50 p.m.
10 hours and 40 minutes
56.81 miles

The Trail
Colorado

GDMBR Day 27
August 12, Friday

Weather—Sun, cool, partly cloudy
Aspen Alley, WY, to Clark, CO (home)

John's Notes: We have been looking forward to this day for the last week. The idea of seeing our family, friends, and dog motivates us more than ever. However, 62 miles biking in Colorado is never easy.

I can smell the ranch.

We are more than excited to enter Colorado this morning, especially seeing Barney and Krista as they drop off our friend Mark! Our route this morning is on pavement to start and mostly downhill, and for the first time in days my leg does not feel sore. As we get started, there are no issues.

Around 9:00 a.m. we reach the planned meeting spot, a bridge close to the Slater Post Office. We made it to Colorado. Mark brings energy and something new to the trail. We all hold hands as Mark says a quick prayer. He asks God to show mercy on him, as he tests his mind, spirit, and body. The air is crisp, and it feels like fall.

Our first goal of the day is to make Brush Mountain Lodge for lunchtime. We'd read about their hospitality to GDMBR bikers. As we ride up to the lodge, we are worried that it looks closed. We walk up to the front door and can hear two women talking. Thank God, they are open. Kristin, the owner, greets all of us with a big hug and offers us breakfast, while her mom gets coffee and tea delivered to us on the porch. Not so bad for Mark's first day on the trail.

The lodge is amazing, and if we didn't have friends and Nina waiting for us at our ranch, we would have spent the night and just stopped there for the day. Still, we are only 30 miles from our home, and we hear it calling us.

We have only one obstacle in the way: a tough mountain climb, Sand Mountain. The climb is really hard, and it becomes clear that Mark is suffering from the altitude and possibly lack of training.

John takes the lead up the hill, and I stay behind with Mark. At a few points on the climb, it is so steep that we have to get off and push our bikes. I almost fall over a number of times as I push my bike up that rocky hill. After 16 miles of intense hill climbing, Mark and I hear John send a *woot woot* our way, meaning he had made the summit. We take a few minutes at the summit to stop, eat, and give our bodies some fuel for the remainder of the trip. Never has a peanut-butter-and-jelly sandwich tasted so good.

From the summit we speed down the hill and approach our ranch. Barney and our friend John Farnam ride their mountain bikes out to meet us on Highway 129—just two miles from our home. We bike into the ranch like a peloton, John and John in front, then Barney, then Mark and me. When we get to the driveway, our children, John and Michelle, are waiting for us with Hillary (our son's girlfriend), Krista, and Paul (John Farnam's husband), and our dog, Nina. I am overwhelmed with love from my friends and family.

After getting off our bikes, we maintain our routine and unpack. We get into our swimsuits and take a cold plunge in the pond. Our family and friends have a huge dinner prepared. They have tons of questions about the trip and we enjoy looking back. With Nina, our dog, snuggled into bed with us, it is nice to know we are home—for the time being.

Ending day stats:

Start 7:20 a.m. Finish 6:45 p.m.
11 hours and 25 minutes
62.73 miles

August 13
Saturday

Rest day—OFF

Today we take a rest day off from biking and just enjoy everyone. We spend the day stand-up paddleboarding at Pearl Lake. My daughter seems amused with the tan lines on my legs and on my fingers. I have worn three-quarter pants for the entire journey, so the only exposed skin during the rides are my calves and the tips of my fingers. Everyone keeps commenting on how skinny we are. We haven't really noticed until getting home.

We spend the day eating a lot of good food and sharing tales from the trail—from our first days in the beauty of the Canadian Rockies through the last days of crossing the windswept Great Basin of Wyoming. I close my eyes for the night with Nina snuggling close.

My leg is feeling much better after just one day off, and I have decided I will be able to go on.

GDMBR Day 28
August 14, Sunday

End of week four
Weather—Sun, warm
Clark to Steamboat Springs, CO

John's Notes: In order to give our bodies one extra day of rest, we agree to bike from our ranch, in Clark, to Steamboat Springs, about 30 miles and mostly downhill. We hope to get back to our 50- to 70-mile days, but today we want to just take it easy and enjoy the day in Steamboat, our favorite mountain town in Colorado.

A late start and a lazy river day.

It's Sunday morning and all our guests pack up and leave. We say goodbye to Barney and Krista, as they are off to the Bonneville Salt Flats in Utah. After a short eight miles, we stop at the Clark General Store for lunch. The Clark Store is on the GDMBR and intersects with both the main route over Sand Mountain and the alternative route on Highway 129. After a laid-back lunch, we get back in the saddle and head down Elk River Road toward Steamboat. Shortly after departing, we come across two other Divide Riders who are doing the ride as journalists and interviewing riders along the way; we are, of course, happy to share our story.

Soon enough, we're in Steamboat Springs, biking along the Yampa River. Families are tubing down the river, and people are just enjoying the summer day. We bike through town for a bit until we reach Howelsen Hill, where some of the world-class skiers and snowboarders train during the summer and winter. It brings back recent memories of watching the University of Denver ski team win the NCAA Championship earlier in the year.

Mark needs to get a few things fixed on his bike, and John wants to get my pannier fixed as well. We choose to stay at Rabbit Ears Motel for the night, for the location is right in the heart of town. We head to the Yampa River for a plunge in the cool water and spend some time in the hot springs that open into the river. We are able to walk to dinner from the motel and enjoy good wine and good pizza at Mambo Italiano. There's even enough left over for me to box up so that we can have a pizza lunch on the trail tomorrow.

By the end of the day, I am already excited about getting back on track. Resting for a day and a half has helped my leg recuperate. It feels like it's back to 100 percent. At one point it was getting so bad that I'd contemplated stopping at our ranch in Clark and letting John bike across Colorado with Mark. However, after taking the time to let my leg heal, I am ready to continue.

Ending day stats:
Start 12:20 p.m. Finish 3:45 p.m.
3 hours and 25 minutes
27.66 miles

GDMBR Day 29
August 15, Monday

Weather—Sun, cool to hot
Steamboat Springs to Radium Campground, CO

John's Notes: With no Continental Divide crossing, but an appreciation for the rugged nature of the Colorado Rockies, we set our goal to one of the two Radium Campgrounds, a popular rafting launch-site on the Colorado River.

And then there were three . . .

We are now three, so the energy has changed. Mark is enthusiastic and ready for the day. We start our morning early in the crisp mountain air; we can tell that fall is on the way. Soon after leaving Steamboat Springs we are in horse country. At a small ranch we see twin colts. They are so darn cute I have to stop. They come immediately over to the fence and let me scratch behind their ears. As we continue to ride south, we discover the rolling hills, pastures, and more small ranches. Approaching the valley floor, we continue along a picturesque river with fly fishermen at every turn. As the miles roll by, we are already talking about returning to this very spot, with friends, when our journey is over.

We stop for lunch at an aspen grove along the road, overlooking a pond and a small ranch. We share the pizza from last night's dinner and finish lunch with a raspberry bar from the Clark General Store. I regrettably had forgotten Michelle's vegan lasagna in the refrigerator at the ranch, so we will have to eat the processed food I have instead of homemade.

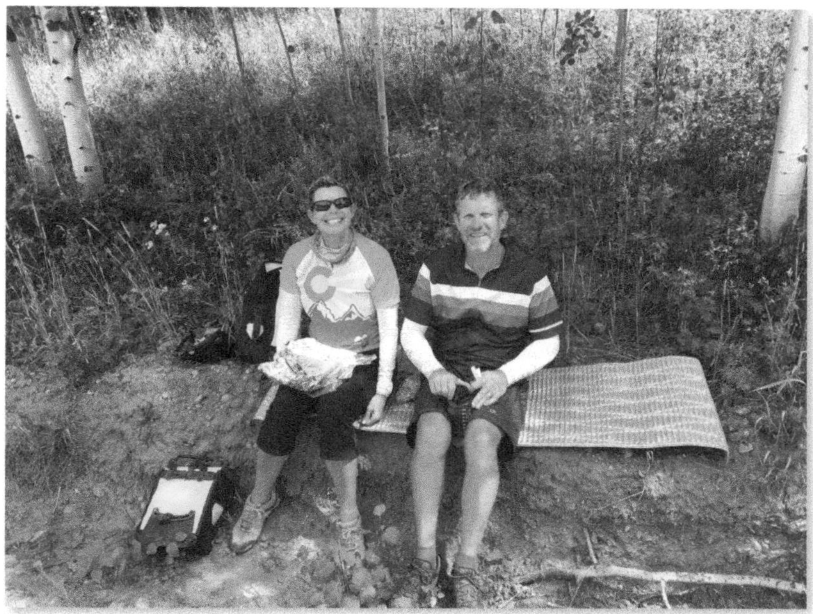

The hill climb we have on the way out of our lunch spot is steep, just as we expected, considering we are in mountainous Colorado. After 20 minutes of climbing, we are able to look down and see the lake where we had just enjoyed lunch. Near the top of the hill we come across some wild raspberries—which of course we have to stop and eat. So far, the Colorado section has been easier than I thought it would be—picturesque and gradual hill climbs. My leg seems to be fine, and I have had no pain in over 24 hours.

Around 2:00 p.m. the rain comes down as it typically does in the afternoons of Colorado summers, and we are happy to be cooled off. The route brings steep climbs and descents as well. I spot a red fox near the top of one of the hills, and he seems to be eating something. The fox could not care less about us until I go to take his picture, and then he runs away.

There is a long descent down a rocky, steep road after leaving the fox. We can see the river below where we will be camping for the night, and we are excited to get there. However, even though we thought we had a nice descent the rest of the way, we soon hit one more hill climb. Mark and I bitch about the climb and blame John, as we are convinced we were supposed to just be coasting the whole way into camp, and that John took us the wrong way.

Reaching the first Radium Campsite, our intended destination, we are all spent. We have a snack and use the bathrooms before planning to move on to the next campground. However, after talking with some local campers, we decide to stay put. We set up camp along the river and prepare for the darkness and the cold by gathering wood for a fire. We each take a bath in the freezing-cold river. It does revitalize our bodies and washes off some of the stink.

After the sun sets, aggressive mosquitoes come out in full force. They sting us over and over. Dousing myself in bug spray does no good. The river close by is certainly the perfect place for these critters to live and breed. After we build a fire, the onslaught seems to slow. John and I begin cooking dinner with our small propane stove. Because we left Michelle's homemade lasagna back at the ranch, we are stuck with lentil soup and rice for dinner. I have enough for all of us.

The night brings freight trains rolling by at all hours. We discover that trains whistle their horns at all intersections; this includes the intersection at the bridge where we built our campsite. Mark doesn't sleep a wink. Maybe it's from the cold, or the train, or the thin air. It is the total opposite for us. Our minds and bodies are now accustomed to the hard ground; with the cold, we just put our coats over our faces and fall into deep sleep.

While we've had 27 other days to get used to the GDMBR, Mark has not. We can feel how hard it is to join this kind of journey halfway through.

Ending day stats:

Start 7:20 a.m. Finish 5:00 p.m.
9 hours and 40 minutes
60.13 miles

GDMBR Day 30
August 16, Tuesday

Weather—Sun, cool to hot, rain
Radium to Silverthorne, CO

John's Notes: Despite a tough four-mile climb out of Radium and Ute Pass later in the day, we are all driven to continue our progress forward to get to the finish. A soft hotel bed and a hot shower provide extra motivation.

Almost four seasons in one day.

Today is the coldest morning so far. John starts a fire while we break down our campsite and get breakfast started—hot water and oatmeal for John and Mark, and a bagel with PB&J for me. We always start our camping mornings with hot water for tea. We huddle next to the fire and eat our meals, preparing our minds for the day ahead.

In the middle of the night, Mark struggled to find his inhaler. He had a hard night, with the cold and difficulty of his asthma. We helped him get reorganized, refocused, and refueled.

It is literally freezing cold this morning. I have on all three coats, my bike gloves and my warm gloves, and my bike pants and rain pants. The steep climb out of Radium seems to take us about two hours. By the time we are finishing climbing out of the canyon, I have my mind set on food. I am very hungry. There is a Subway in Kremmling, and I am totally focused on getting there. When we get to Subway, we eat a breakfast sandwich and order a footlong sandwich for lunch, because we know there is a tough pass ahead of us. After packing up the extra food, we venture across the street and hit the local coffee shop for a sweet treat of homemade cinnamon buns and fresh-baked pastries. Our final stop is at the gas station for snacks and food we can use to refuel on the trail.

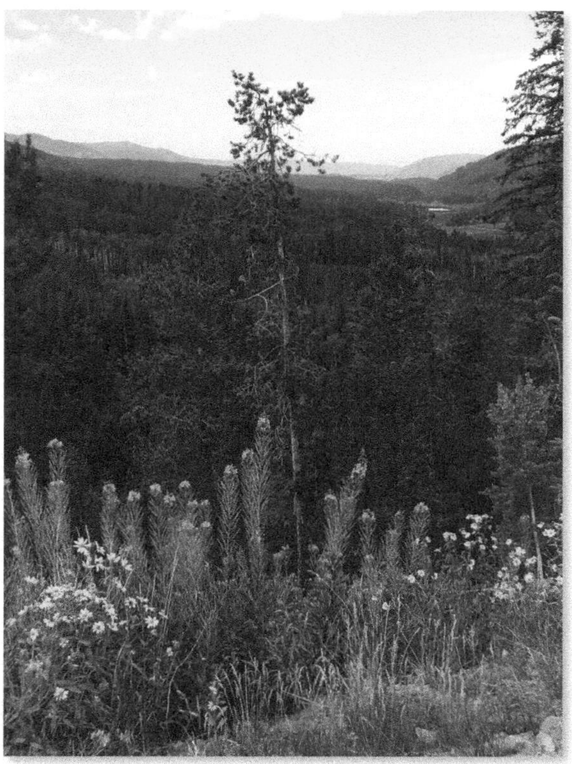

Our goal for the day is to make it to Silverthorne, where hotels and restaurants are abundant; because we don't leave Kremmling until 11:00 a.m., I doubt we'll make it. However, by the way John pushes himself, and subsequently us, it's rather obvious that Silverthorne is still the goal. We put our heads down and spin, as the sun rises higher in the sky.

The pass approaches . . .

We take a late lunch stop along the road after our first choice doesn't work due to an air assault from swarming ants that resemble termites—I have never seen anything like it. Anyway, we eventually make it to a safe location and take out our sandwiches.

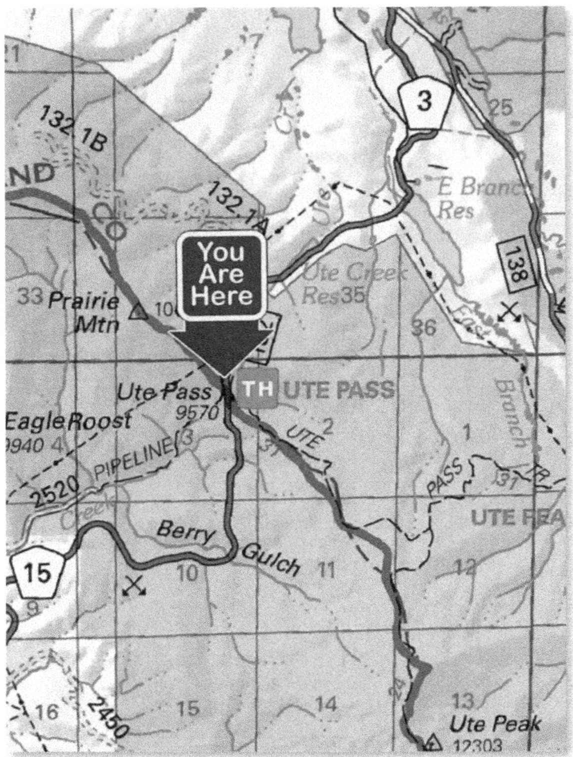

The farther we climb up the pass, the farther Mark falls behind. We stop several times to cheer him on. The asthma and altitude are taking their toll. Eventually, we all summit the Ute Pass. After the tough climb, we are rewarded by a steep downhill that lets us pick up some impressive speeds. At the bottom of the hill, we are jettisoned onto Highway 9 with just 13 miles left until Silverthorne.

I have never biked this section of the road before, but I am very familiar with the route, as John and I drive it all the time on our way to our ranch. One thing you don't notice in the car is that the entire way to Silverthorne is a gradual steady climb. With just a few miles to go, the rest of the day should be a breeze—but we are met with a steady headwind, and our tired bodies struggle to make good time.

John takes the lead and cuts the headwind for me, but Mark is unable to take advantage of our drafting formation. He is having a hard time breating and is lacking air so badly that he can't even talk. John and I begin to worry, as Mark's asthma seems to be getting worse. We continue to stop and cheer him on until we reach Silverthorne.

I am able to find two hotel rooms for us at the Hampton Inn & Suites. After John and I get situated, we call Mark for dinner. "I'll catch up with you at the restaurant," he tells us. So we head out for dinner without him.

He never shows up.

I call him during dinner but his phone goes to voicemail. Later we find out that Mark has gone to the emergency room. We truly didn't realize the severity of Mark's health issues. I regret not asking him before we left if he had anything that might pose a health risk. Concerned for Mark's health, we wonder if he should continue.

Ending day stats:

Start 7:25 a.m. Finish 7:25 p.m.
12 hours
73.01 miles

GDMBR Day 31
August 17, Wednesday

Weather—Sun to overcast, rain, hail
Silverthorn to Hartsel, CO

John's Notes: Having done longer-term trail planning with Mark back at our ranch, we had been able to stay on schedule. The plan was to cross Boreas Pass, elevation 11,482 feet, and make it to Hartsel for today's daily goal. Our concern was on Mark, and we needed to talk with him before departure.

It's a marathon, not a sprint.

This is the theme of our journey—tackle each day with its new challenges; consider what's important and what we can let go. Push ourselves only as hard as is necessary.

At the hotel, Mark joins us for breakfast. He is surprisingly excited for the day, considering he spent the night in the emergency room. Today is a big decision for him—will his lungs allow him to keep pushing, or is he going to have to stop? Mark knows he needs to put his health before his dream of biking across Colorado.

We talk about what the doctor said when Mark went to the emergency room. The doctor sees many East Coast riders who live at sea level. When they try to push hard at altitude, they often end up in the ER. Fortunately for Mark, his decision to keep biking will be dependent on a few factors: specifically while climbing hills he has to be able to breathe and talk; and if at any time the pressure on his chest gets to the point where it feels like a huge weight is there, then the ride is a no-go.

We start our morning on the bike path that runs between Silverthorne, Dillon, Frisco, and Breckenridge. We experience the most beautiful views of Dillon Reservoir and the surrounding mountains. We aren't the only ones enjoying the early-morning sun and crisp mountain air. I am able to capture a few photos of some baby geese. I must have gotten too close, as the mother goose hisses at me, flashing her red tongue.

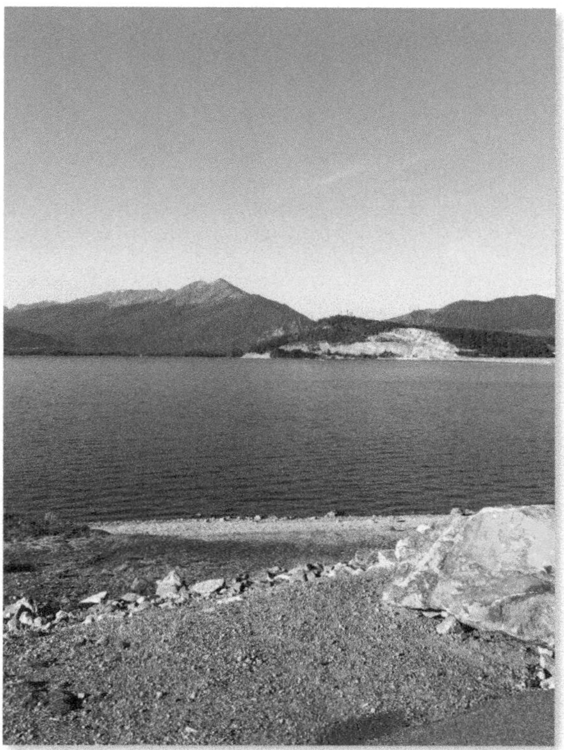

We restock our food supply in Breckenridge.

At 10:30 a.m. we meet our first challenge of the day, which is a good test for Mark's asthma as well—Boreas Pass, the second-highest crossing on our entire journey. The road starts out paved and is a gradual climb to begin. Mark drops back early, listening to doctor's orders—take the hills at his pace, not ours.

The road turns to dirt, and we stop to wait for Mark at the transition from smooth pavement to choppy dirt road. His face looks stricken as he rides up to us and says, "This is it. I have to say goodbye." He gets off his bike and immediately sinks to his knees, tears streaming down his face. He had put hours of research into this trip and had bought all new equipment. Instead of a 50th birthday party, this bike ride and the equipment was his gift to himself—and now he has to call it quits because his body won't allow him to continue.

The sprint is over. He's choosing the marathon of life—for his wife and children. He's already called his wife. She immediately hopped on a plane to Denver and would be in Breckenridge in a few short hours. Mark would bike back and meet her there. We wouldn't have gone any farther if Mark's wife wasn't already on her way. We know that Mark is actively talking with a local doctor, and we feel he'll be all right.

Mark had been the only friend to accept our challenge to bike with us. He added energy, love, fun, and so much more. Now, it's back to the two of us, back on the road a little sooner than we anticipated. Adjusting to the new rhythm is difficult at first, as we already miss our friend.

From where we left Mark, the rest of the hill climb is gradual because the road used to be a railroad track. The climb is serene and striking. We eventually reach the summit and are met with warm greetings from three motorcycle gentlemen. We enjoy lunch with them and share stories, comparing the difference between motorcycling and biking the pass. They have just ridden up from Como, the next town on our map. They let us know that there is not much there. All three men are from Denver and belong to a club that shoots guns on Thursdays and rides motorcycles on Tuesdays. Retirement is a fine life, and their club sounds like quite a bit of fun. As we're finishing lunch, the sky turns dark and the wind begins to swirl. We say goodbyes and each head our separate ways.

The clouds look menacing, and we know that lightning, thunder, hail, and rain are all a possibility. On our descent, the sky cracks and rumbles and opens up. When the rain turns to hail, we stop to take cover under some trees, even though we are cautious of hiding under trees when lightning is brightening a dark afternoon sky. The temperature drops quickly, and we have to throw on some layers of clothes to keep warm while we wait out the heavy part of the storm. After 30 minutes or so, the hail stops, but the rain continues. With our rain gear on, we descend down the pass.

Our fingers are totally frozen but we continue to bike as fast as possible. The quicker we can get off the pass, the quicker we'll warm up.

Finally, we reach the town of Como. The bikers we met at the top of the pass were right; there is nothing but a post office located, for some strange reason, in the back of an art gallery. We head inside for cover as the lightning, thunder, and rain continue. The woman working the post office tells us that Hartsel, a town 30 miles away, has food and a lodge. According to her, it's all downhill.

That is not the case . . .

From Como to Hartsel the topography changes from mountainous beauty to rolling plains. Our freezing bodies begin to warm up, and we reach Hartsel three hours after leaving Como. We're happy to find that the cafe is open and that we can get a hot dinner. A local customer helps me get the phone number to the Hartsel Lodge, and we are able to book a room for the night. After dinner we have to put our wet rain gear back on as the lodge is two miles away and the rain has not subsided.

The lodge is a sight to behold as we enter an old mansion that has been completely restored. It turns out that we are the only guests. It is so nice, I am worried about our dirty bikes on their floors, so I unpack everything on some extra towels the manager has given me. After taking a hot shower, I call to check in on Mark. His wife is there and they have fallen in love with the town of Breckenridge. Mark's voice does not improve, but his spirits are high and he is slowly feeling better.

Each day our marathon journey has ups and downs. It's how we get from A to B. Supporting each other in any way we can along the trail and embracing the surprises—like the lodge—make this journey so magical. From the emotional drain of leaving Mark behind, almost freezing in a hail storm, and then biking several hours to get to the next spot just so we can sleep in a real bed—well, the feeling is beyond words, really.

Ending day stats:

Start 7:40 a.m. Finish 7:10 p.m.
11 hours and 30 minutes
72.42 miles

GDMBR Day 32
August 18, Thursday

Weather—Sun to rain
Hartsel to Salida, CO

John's Notes: Our goal for today is Salida, Colorado, where we are to meet our good friends, who are our neighbors in Florida.

On the trail, old friends to new friends can lift the spirit.

There is not a cloud in the sky when we wake up in our big, comfortable bed. Today motivation is high with much to look forward to. First, our next stop in Salida is the home of our dear friends John and Carol Wagner, who have made arrangements for us to spend the night on their ranch with them. We only have to bike 50 miles today, which is pretty short in comparison to some of our previous days.

The start of the day is very chilly, and when the sun finally comes up, it feels great. Today's ride starts in the plains. Quickly we reach our first pass. It's a relatively easy climb, and at the top we stop for lunch next to a stream. As we're wrapping our lunch up, two Divide Riders from Australia stop, and we chat for a while. They are on their way to Hartsel Lodge after taking a day's rest in Salida. We share our awesome experience with them.

On our way down the pass, we see cowboys and cowgirls moving cattle up the hill. It's a slow and steady trek as they gently prod the cattle to move along. We can see Salida on the horizon. There are gray and black clouds looming over the city. We witness lightning strike after lightning strike. Through the sun streaks highlighted in the clouds, the rain bursts are very apparent; we wonder which rain burst we might be biking through on our way into town. We meet our friends at the grocery, an easy point for both of us to find, and they drive us to their beautiful ranch.

Upon arrival, we are welcomed by Chance, their dog. Chance and Nina, our dog, are friends; they've gone on many beach walks with us in Florida. The Wagners' home is artistic, starting at the front door and all the way throughout. Carol has purchased tons of fresh food for us, so as we unpack and do laundry, we enjoy the hearty platters of appetizers. The rain continues to fall for the rest of the night, so we can't explore their property. While Carol is cooking in the kitchen, we share our stories from the GDMBR and talk about Mark. We wish he could have been there with us. We enjoy a truly great evening with John and Carol and finish our meal with homemade chocolate cake.

After dinner, I call to check on Mark. He says his lungs feel like he has been punched in the gut and lost his breath, and that his voice is still gone. When his wife got there, they drove the Boreas Pass. He tells me, "I made the right decision. After driving that climb, I see my lungs would not have made it."

I'm sad he's struggling, but happy to know that he is safe and recovering. He is feeling well enough to explore the town and the pass—he just has to do it from the comfort of their rental car.

Ending day stats:

Start 8:25 a.m. Finish 3:05 p.m.
6 hours 40 minutes
50.39 miles

GDMBR Day 33
August 19, Friday

Weather—Sun, wind
Salida to Upper Dome Campsite, CO

John's Notes: We are determined to make it to Del Norte, which is 150 miles away. This will take us two days, so we set our sights on Upper Dome Campsite—about halfway to our goal.

Determination and perseverance bring the finish line closer.

The alarm rings early at 5:30 a.m. because today is going to be longer than yesterday, with some tougher biking to boot. It's always great to get a good night's sleep whenever you're pushing yourself. The bed is so comfortable and warm it's really hard to get out of it and brave the cold morning.

Today is Marshall Pass and we want to stay ahead of the rain. We start the day with blue sky. We want to come back and ride our dirt bikes with them, have time to hang out and just chill. Carol and John get up extra early with us and drive us back close to the spot where we met them the day prior.

The climb is mild on the dirt road, which allows us to talk and enjoy the scenery. A doe and her two fawns are exposed on one of our first turns. She alertly watches us as we ride by, ensuring her two young ones are safe. While steadily climbing, we notice a beautiful campsite that overlooks a lake, surrounded by bike trails. We have read that the single track in this area is one of the best in Colorado, not only because it's amazing in and of itself, but also because it's surrounded by more awesome bike trails. In short, we are definitely coming back.

We find a couple of rusted railroad spikes and stop to pick them up because they are old, rare, and pretty darn cool; we don't mind carrying them for the rest of the trip. A group of mountain sheep is up ahead on the trail, eating something from a small hole in the middle of the road. We get very close to them before they run and hide in the brush. We stop just after passing the hole they are eating from, and I am able to capture them running back to the same spot to finish what they were eating.

We summit Marshall Pass about three hours after leaving John and Carol. We don't wait at the top of the pass for too long, as we know how quickly the weather can change and we don't want to get caught in the rain. At the bottom of the pass, we are abruptly jettisoned out of sweeping vistas and the cool shade cast by the towering shadows of trees and into plains and scrub brush marred by the ever-consistent beating down of sun during the summer and cold wind during the winter.

Racing down the hill, we catch a glimpse of a Great Divide map in the middle of the dirt road. Shortly after, we meet a young man who lost his map. He asks if we've seen it, so we're able to direct him back to it. He's on day 42 of his GDMBR journey. We are on day 33, putting us nine days faster than he. He says he's from Cincinnati, Ohio, and he is determined to finish the GDMBR. We wish we had picked up the map, as we could have ridden with him for a couple of days. Instead, he turns around and heads back up the hill to retrieve his map. We never see him again. After we leave him, we talk about how fortunate we are to have each other, and wonder if either one of us could have made it this far on our own.

Sargents, Colorado, is the next town on our map. It is a small town, with a gas station with a restaurant and an unnamed campground, located directly on Highway 50. We stop at the gas station and cafe for lunch. The cook is familiar with GDMBR bikers coming through and offers us unlimited ice and to-go cups filled with water. When we tell the chef that we don't eat meat, she looks at us both like we are crazy. I order a big dinner salad and a cheeseburger with no burger and no cheese. She stops midway through the process of taking my order and stares at me for a quick second before telling me that she "can't do that."

I tell her I'll do a grilled cheese—I am so hangry that I'll eat the damn cheese. She returns a few moments after taking my order and tells me that she can sauté some mushrooms and onions and add a tomato to my sandwich as well, so in the end I get a tasty meal, even if it has cheese on it.

After lunch, we only have to bike 12 miles on Highway 50, then get back on a county road for a 25-mile ride to our campground. The highway is crazy busy with Friday afternoon traffic. We are passed by a group of Corvettes rumbling along the freeway, no doubt heading to some car meet or gathering of sorts. All of this activity jars us a bit—it's tough to get used to people all around you when you're used to seeing so few humans over so many days. Luckily the activity subsides as soon as we make our turn onto the county road and start heading to our campsite.

The last 25 miles is pretty difficult, with long hills and views that extended for miles without any vegetation in sight. At 5:00 p.m., when the route seems harder and harder, we decide to take a break and drink our beloved Crystal Light Peach tea with ice water in our red jug and share a Pop-Tart. Taking a few minutes for a rest stop—giving fuel to the body—always seems to carry us to the end of the day.

As we approach the Upper Dome Campsites, I can see an outhouse structure and some campers. The closer we get, the more my mental fortitude is challenged. Furthermore, I can see where we're headed, and that we are going to have to bike up the reservoir first before backtracking to a campsite. This will add a few miles to our already long day. However, after we get to the reservoir, we see another outhouse and a water pump station. We opt to pitch our tent rather than biking to the other campsite a few more miles away. The campsite is on the road, but there is not a lot of traffic. John is worried about the rainstorms above us, and thinks we could possibly get snow if the clouds produce water.

Dinner is vegetarian canned chili and rice. Carol had insisted we take a bag of gold Hershey's kisses, so we savor the tasty chocolate treat at the end of a long day. We are happy to have made it through another day with no injuries, without getting lost, and to have climbed another pass.

We hit the hard ground for the night's rest and are serenaded to sleep by the howling of a cold wind and the yipping of coyotes.

Ending day stats:

Start 7:50 a.m. Finish 6:15 p.m.
10 hours and 25 minutes
68.53 miles

GDMBR Day 34
August 20, Saturday

Weather—Sun, cool, overcast
Upper Dome Reservoir to Del Norte, CO

John's Notes: We knew our goal of reaching Del Norte in two days would be challenging. With two high mountain passes to cross, we knew it was going to be a tough day—but with the prospect of a hotel in Del Norte, our spirits were high.

2,000 miles on a mountain bike is a long way!

I had plans to meet my mom and stepdad, Ken, in Del Norte on Sunday; today is Saturday. With our determined pace this means we will miss them by one day. My mom lives in Montrose, Colorado, which is not too far from Del Norte. When I get cell reception and call to ask if they can come one day early, my mom tells me that she has already committed to a hospital charity event, and that she can't back out now. She encourages us to keep pressing, saying, "I don't want to hold you back."

So we decide to keep our pace. As we enter Gunnison National Forest, the beauty of the natural stone takes our breath away.

Today is extra special because we hit 2,000 miles on the GDMBR and 2,650 in total miles biked, if you include our training miles! For every 100 miles we bike, I have been ringing my bike bell. (Back when we trained for those initial 650 miles, I rang it every 50 miles!) Today there is extra bell-ringing and celebrating.

From my marathon days, for each mile I ran, I would dedicate one mile to someone special in my life. Celebrating small accomplishments is my way of reaching big goals or dreams.

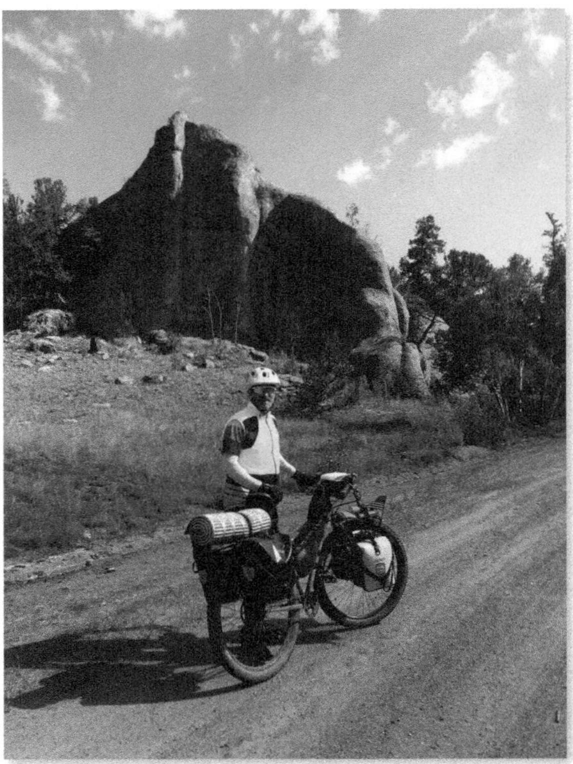

Today's route is truly stunning, as we bike in and out of the Rio Grande National Forest. The beauty of the rock formations makes me want to learn more about the changes they go through over the millions of years it takes for them to form. Like so many other areas we've seen along the way, we want to come back to this area, as there is so much to see and explore.

We struggle through the last two miles of the trip with spent legs and a depleted mental fortitude that has been slowly chiseled away throughout the course of the day. Today was truly beautiful, but it was long; by 5:30 p.m., we are totally exhausted. On a Saturday night the Windsor Hotel has one room, and we take it, realizing how lucky we are. It was once the center of the town and known for its grandeur. The hotel had fallen on tough times until it was recently restored. I read the plaques on the wall about how many local citizens had come together to pay for the restoration. The art is grand and the room we are in has been perfectly restored. Because of the beautiful restoration our bikes are not allowed in our room—something we completely understand. They lock up our bikes in a storage room, and we take our panniers, like luggage, to our room.

After a long hot shower we head downstairs to the bar. Kevin, the bartender, is incredibly personable. He can tell right away that we are GDMBR bikers, and he shares stories with us about other Divide Riders and about the local area. He convinces us to dine in the bar and hang out with him. The wine he picks for me is perfect, and after three baskets of their homemade delicious bread, our first course arrives. Dinner is grilled salmon, with roasted potatoes and spinach, and each bite melts in my mouth. We watch the summer Olympics and the Denver Broncos while we eat—the perfect duo. If you find yourself in Del Norte, the Windsor Hotel is not to be missed—make sure to say hi to Kevin for us!

Ending day stats:

Start 7:20 a.m. Finish 5:30 p.m.
10 hours and 10 minutes
71.21 miles

GDMBR Day 35
August 21, Sunday

End of week five
Weather—Overcast, cool, rain
Del Norte to Platoro, CO

John's Notes: Platoro is our biker friendly next stop, about 50 miles away. However, Indiana Pass is a 24-mile hill climb, with more than 4,000 vertical feet of uphill.

Indiana Pass is the highest point on the route at 11,910 feet!

We had planned on sleeping in a bit, but at 5:45 a.m. we are wide-awake. By day 35 of our adventure, we have clearly trained ourselves to get an early start—and we are ready to go. After packing up, we walk down the street to the local cafe for breakfast.

During breakfast we talk about taking the day off. We were, after all, supposed to meet my mom and stepdad here today, so we might as well wait for them. Alas, the reunion is not meant to be. I am unable to find an open hotel room anywhere in Del Norte, so onward we must go.

By the time we check out of the hotel, the sky has turned from sunny to stormy, and we still have to go to the grocery store for supplies and stop at Subway for our lunch. Even though we got up super early, we end up getting a really late start. With this late start comes anxiety, and I feel behind.

We have one important call that we have to make while we have cell service—a call to Barney and Krista. We have been preparing to return to Denver for a surprise wedding. Barney and Krista are headed south to meet us. We need to confirm where we think we might be before departing Del Norte. John is able to reach Barney, and they decide where to pick us up. Barney has a really good feel for where we are and how many miles we are averaging each day. It sounds as if we should be able to intersect sometime Tuesday afternoon.

Once we finally start the day, we immediately encounter an 11-mile hill climb, which forces us into a slow start on the 50 miles we have to go. The sky grows darker, and John says we may have to turn back if the lightning comes too close to us. He, too, feels behind and shares with me that the guidebook said to get an early start. Well, we botched that; now I feel even more anxious.

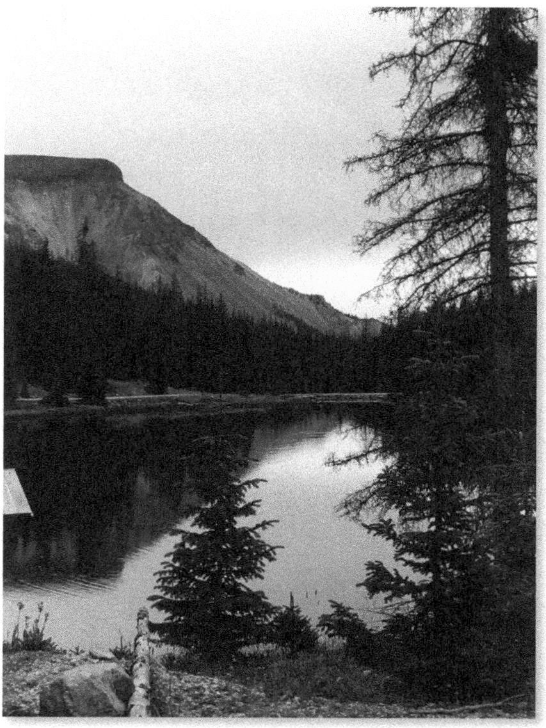

As the pavement turns to dirt and the pitch of the road changes right along with it, things get a lot steeper. The book and elevation chart on the map warned us of this, but Colorado has been fairly easy so far and we just assumed today would be the same. Obviously we hadn't done our nightly homework as we usually do. The hotel, good food, and tasty wine had made us a bit too comfortable, and now we are paying the price.

By 4:30 p.m. we have only biked 18 miles. The weather is still holding formation in a dark sky without dropping much rain, but it looks like it might pour. We feel lucky, because it feels like it has been raining everywhere around us, but not on us. We hear thunder and see lightning at a reasonable distance from us, so we keep climbing. Shortly after we summit Indiana Pass, we bike through the abandoned mining town of Summitville. There is a massive effort to mitigate the pollution from the former mine. It's the site of a Superfund Cleanup for the EPA—something I have never seen before.

We continue to climb, but we need fuel. We eat the second half of our sandwich and the chocolates that Carol Wagner insisted I take—I am happy she insisted. As we come over the next hill, we see the most beautiful mountains of shale. Filled with iron, the red and rust colors dominate the hillside. Even though the sky is gray, we are still able to see the sheer beauty of the mountains, and we promise ourselves that we will return.

Only 5 miles to go . . .

But, 6:00 p.m. has come and gone. And then 7:00 p.m.

Where is Platoro? Is our mileage off?

It seems like we'll never get there . . .

The sun has now set and we are biking in the dark, headed down a rocky and bumpy road, which makes it even harder.

At last we arrive—utterly relieved to have made it. As we walk up to the lodge in the dark, we can hear people inside. Two dogs bark at the sound of our approach.

The sign says CLOSED.

John knocks on the door, and we wait . . .

Thankfully, a girl opens the door. We tell her we are Divide Riders, and she welcomes us in with a hearty greeting, "All bikers are welcome here!" There is a roaring fire, and the two dogs that were barking welcome us with friendly tail wags and dog smiles.

Unfortunately, we have missed dinner at the cafe due to our late arrival. Thankfully, they have a small wall stocked with food for cabin renters like us. Our cabin is rustic and charming. While John starts a fire, I start dinner. We have never biked in the dark before tonight, and we haven't biked past 8:00 p.m., either. I'm sure it won't be the last time, but we did learn our lesson—it's best to get up and just get going.

Ending day stats:

Start 11:15 a.m. Finish 8:05 p.m.
8 hours and 50 minutes
49.28 miles

The Trail

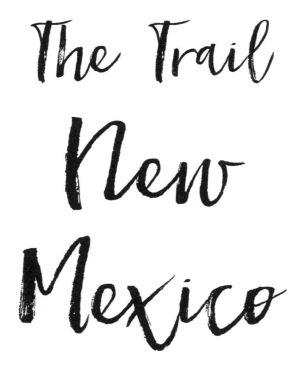

New Mexico

GDMBR Day 36
August 22, Monday

Weather—Sun, overcast, rain
Platoro, CO, to Lower Lagunitas Campground, NM

John's Notes: We have scheduled to meet Barney and Krista on Tuesday. Having had a long and difficult day yesterday, we decide to ride to Lower Lagunitas Campground, leaving only 35 miles for tomorrow where the trail and Highway 64 would intersect.

When riding the Great Divide, it's best to order two of the world's largest pancakes.

After a great night's sleep in the old rustic cabin, I can't sleep past 5:30 a.m. I make tea on the rustic stove and wait for John to get up. He wakes up not too long after the kettle starts its whistle. We decide to go back to bed until the cafe opens at 7:00 a.m.

The cafe is something fun and special. John and I both order the pancakes—John orders a triple-decker, and I order a double-decker. Our waitress tells us that their pancakes are pretty big, and that one pancake each is probably enough. John keeps his triple order, and I downsize to just one, in case they really are that big—we are skeptical.

Let me make something very clear: These pancakes must be engineered in a lab somewhere off-location, because I have never seen a pancake like this one—they really are that big. I eat as much as I possibly can and get the rest to go. Meanwhile, John can only eat a small portion, so I get his portion to go, too.

After just a few miles of pedaling, our legs are incredibly tired. Thankfully the first 20 miles to Horca are all downhill. The view on the downhill ride is spectacular, and the road is next to a stream. The sun rises as we continue to descend, and the mountains come alive, touched by the early-morning glow.

The town of Horca is small and über-cute. Our map and book have indicated that we can stock up on food at a small convenience store on our way out of town. However, we are told that the store has closed down. Since then, another small store on the route has tried to stock up on food items. Unfortunately, we find this store has mostly trinkets and knickknacks. Their food selection is limited to sugar treats and items with meat. We buy some homemade cinnamon rolls and candy and head on our way. We will survive for the next 24 hours on our gigantic leftover pancakes. I do have some bagels left, but they are stale and hard.

After leaving Horca, we encounter our first hill climb of the day. The sun is in front of us, and thunderous dark rain clouds loom ominously behind us. The storm catches up with us, soon pouring down. We are able to find respite from the rain under some trees. The top of the pass is frigid, however, so we don't stay long. We descend and pass some ranchers moving their cattle up the hill. This has become a common experience during our journey.

However, the world we live in is far from common, and we are reminded of this when we see a speeding pickup truck barreling toward us on the paved road, with a dog standing on the roof! The dog is barking at us as the truck quickly approaches. As they pass us, the dog jumps off the roof and into the bed of the truck so it can let loose a few more pointed remarks in dog-speak before disappearing over the crest of the hill. John and I turn toward each other, totally speechless. We are undoubtedly thinking the same thing: What just happened? What if the driver had to suddenly brake? What would happen to his dog? There are so many scenarios that could have put the dog's life in jeopardy, and we are clearly shaken. The more I try to put it out of my head, however, the more I keep thinking about it. Life is precious—for humans and animals alike.

Shortly after this crazy encounter, we turn off the paved road and head into the forest. Within an hour we reach the Colorado/New Mexico border. The front wheel of my bike crosses the border, and I immediately climb off my bike, gently letting it hit the ground before walking back into Colorado to take a rest on a nearby rock that is calling my name. The sun feels amazing on the warm rock, and a chipmunk keeps me entertained. I feel rejuvenated after the rest, and warmed by the rock. We go back to climbing another hill just a few minutes later.

Our goal is to reach the Lower Lagunitas Campground for the night, and rests that take too long are not tolerated! The higher we climb, the more the terrain of the road changes. The trail turns into a muddy, rocky road as we enter the Carson National Forest. When we finally reach the plateau of our climb, my phone chimes: OMG, we have 4G.

We stop and shoot off some quick texts and phone calls. It has been almost three days since we have had any connection to the outside world. It feels great to check in on our loved ones and get some succinct updates on what's happening while we're adventuring through North America.

The top of the plateau is breathtaking. It feels like you can see for thousands of miles in a 360-degree view. Large pine trees are intermittently growing, with grass and scrub brush filling in. The afternoon sky has large puffy clouds, making the view even more spectacular. Some hunters who are scoping out deer for opening day of hunting season stop their truck and chat with us for a few minutes. They had seen us biking earlier in the day and thought we were truly crazy. We talk about where we have biked from and our sleeping accommodations versus theirs. While they describe their warm and cozy cabin, we describe our fabulous tent. They laugh and wish us well. Time to get back to scouting for deer.

After leaving the hunters we are ready to be at our campsite; however, at 6:00 p.m. we are still climbing. By 7:15 the sun is taking its final bow for the day, and we are taking the final turn that leads to our campsite. Unfortunately, it's uphill, and I am pissed off—because I'm tired and

I don't want to bike anymore. John can feel my frustration and pedals ahead. When he gets to the top of the hill he whistles, letting me know it is only a short distance to the end. Upon arriving, we immediately see how special the campsite is: remote, yet it has fire pits with plenty of wood, flat areas good for tents, large trees to sleep under, and a bathroom with running water.

By the time we set camp, change clothes, and start a campfire, it's pitch black; and for the first time on the trip, we have to use our headlamps to navigate the campsite. We stand over the campfire to eat our pancake dinner. We are able to go straight to bed without reviewing the map, because tomorrow we are biking only 37 miles to meet Barney and Krista.

Ending day stats:

Start 9:05 a.m. Finish 7:25 p.m.
10 hours and 20 minutes
52.65 miles

GDMBR Day 37
August 23, Tuesday

Weather—Sun
Lower Lagunitas Campground to Hopewell Lake, NM

John's Notes: Knowing we have a short day to Hopewell Lake, we are excited to get picked up and spend the weekend in Denver.

A short day is a day to enjoy.

We wake up to a beautiful sunny morning. John and I finish the last piece of pancake, which is the remainder of our food, and I leave the campsite still hungry. The morning route is a hilly volcanic road. Mud and water are the dominant features on the trail. Many of the hills are not bikeable, and we have to get off our bikes and walk them.

A section of the route is lined with bright green aspen trees. With the morning sun shining on them, the green seems extra vibrant. As we are biking up a road, we see a critter that turns out to be a fairly large badger. I have never seen a real badger in the wild before, and it sparks a great conversation between us, as John's parents and our daughter all went to University of Wisconsin, and their mascot is the badger.

By noon we are starving and running behind schedule. We are eager to see Barney and Krista for many reasons, beginning with the knowledge that they will have food, ice, cold water, and drinks. They've driven almost 500 miles south of Denver to pick us up—pretty great friends we have!

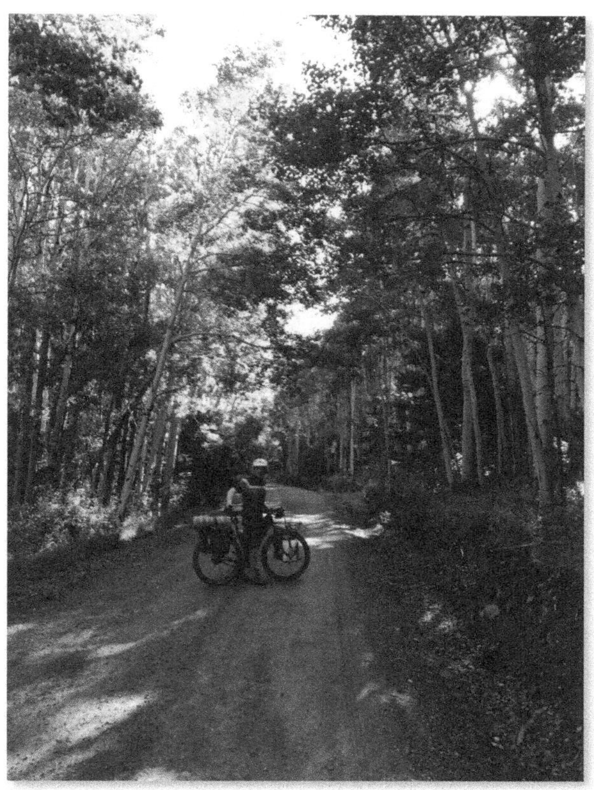

Between Barney's great sense of where we are on the trail, and John's phenomenal directional skills, connecting with them is incredibly easy. If you look at a map of where we meet, you understand how miraculous the pickup truly is.

Ending day stats:
Start 7:35 a.m. Finish 12:05 p.m.
4 hours and 30 minutes
32.6 miles

August 24 to August 27

Weather—sun
Miles—Zero

We don't bike from August 24 to 27.

Taking four days off from the trail might sound awesome, but our goal is to finish. Thus, trying not to get too far out of the rhythm of our routine is going to be hard.

On August 26th we attend John Farnam and Paul Heitzenrater's "surprise wedding." This is why Barney and Krista hung out so long in Colorado after they left us, as we are all close friends and they wanted to attend the wedding with us. We have so much fun celebrating the couple's magical day, not to mention seeing our friends and showing off our newly sculpted hard-bodies.

The next day, on August 27, we celebrate our son's 25th birthday with a family BBQ in his backyard. It's the perfect ending to our time off.

As we say goodbye, our thoughts turn back to the trail, and with four days off, I am afraid we don't seem to have the same fire and determination to finish. Maybe we'll get it back once we put our heads back down and start pedaling.

This is our final goodbye to Barney and Krista, who have given us so much support along the way. It is a summer none of us will ever forget.

GDMBR Day 38
August 28, Sunday

End of week six
Hopewell Lake to Abiquiu, NM

John's Notes: Determined to finish the GDMBR, and knowing we have to drive 500 miles to get back to the trailhead, we set our goal to reach Abiquiu, where there are full services and a hotel reservation in our name.

Rested legs make the biker feel stronger.

Our alarm goes off at 5:00 a.m.; we know that today is going to be a long one. Nate and Michelle, our daughter and her boyfriend, and our dog, Nina, drive us from Denver back to the trailhead where we'd gotten picked up by Barney and Krista. While in Denver, John had our bikes tuned, we rested our legs, John and Paul got married, and our son turned 25—proving that a lot can happen in four days, even if you stay in one place.

At Hopewell Lake, we enjoy an early lunch with our kids. We change back into our GDMBR biking clothes, and as I do this, I can feel the intensity coming back. We must be laser-focused to finish this ride. After four days off, and a return to the comforts we have largely been without, we know it will take some serious mental fortitude to get back into the swing of things.

For the first time in days I am able to get on my bike with zero pain. Everything feels great. However, we are getting a later start than normal and we have 55 miles ahead of us. The ride starts out cool, but soon we are peeling off layers of clothes. The beginning of the ride is in deep, wooded forest. Yet after we crest our first hill and begin the initial descent, we see nothing but desert. Furthermore, we know that the desert will shortly turn into a flood zone and mud, based on what our book has told us—and sure enough, after a few short miles, we are wading through thick and sticky mud. I almost fall off my bike on several different occasions, when my bike gets encased in the sludge.

Biking through the flood zone, you can see the banks of the river and foliage eroding into the steady onslaught of powerful water. The jet stream is causing a monsoonal flow from the Gulf of Mexico, and we are biking right through it—yikes! We know enough about flooding to know that anything can happen at any moment, and so we talk about a safety plan.

We reach the small town of Vallecitos, and while we're taking a break, a nice man strolls by with his three dogs and chats with us about some of the other Divide Riders who have passed through. He loves talking to Divide Riders, he says, and apparently his dogs do as well because they come right up to us and share their dog smiles and kisses. He encourages us to keep pushing, and tells us that after the seven-mile hill climb, it is downhill the rest of the way.

He was totally right. Not only is the remainder of the route downhill after the climb, but it's on a paved road, and we are able to bike at a good speed. John forges ahead so that I can draft with him down the hill. We are biking at 24 miles per hour with 80-pound bikes, and it's obvious that John is pushing harder than normal. He must want to get off the freeway, and I stay close to him. We hold this pace for quite some time, which is strange, given how hard John is pushing. As we make a turn toward the hotel, John says he needs a soda, and we pull off at a pizza place. There is a long line, so we head next door to a bar, where John orders two real Coca-Colas.

He is bonking. He shares with me that he doesn't know how he is going to make it. We talk about setting smaller goals, and our small goal for the rest of the day is to make Abiquiu.

When we reach the destination, we find our room is large but quaint, and we can feel that we are in a very artistic spot. The local restaurant presents food that is artistic and delicious. Everything about New Mexico exudes culture and art. It is a real treat, and we wish we had more time in this town to explore. We look forward to coming back.

Ending day stats:

Start 12:05 p.m. Finish 6:15 p.m.
6 hours and 10 minutes
55.46 miles

GDMBR Day 39
August 29, Monday

Weather—Gray, cold, rain
Abiquiu to a primitive campsite, NM

John's Notes: With the two-day goal of Cuba, New Mexico, we will push as far as we can today. The map indicates a grueling day of climbing, and we hope that the monsoon rains will not slow us down.

Back in the saddle again.

It feels like the trip has started all over again. Even though we only have a few days to go, our mindset isn't that excited to keep going. Everybody on this route will eventually come face-to-face with this moment, and they will have to make a decision as to whether they want to quit or keep moving. In fact, we've encountered this moment many times and kept on trekking, so we know we can do it again.

According to the gentleman at the front desk, the next two days to Cuba, New Mexico, will be brutal. He said, "It is the hardest part of the trail." This is obviously discouraging, and trying to find that little bit of shimmering light in a dark tunnel is difficult.

On our way out of the hotel, in the midst of what we know will be the hardest day yet, we accidentally pass the first turn and continue riding for a few miles in the wrong direction. We just aren't in sync after our four days off. Only a couple of errant miles later, John quickly realizes what has happened and we turn back. Once we make the correct turn onto the rocky red road, we immediately face a steep hill climb. It's so steep that I have to walk my bike. This is going to be yet another long day.

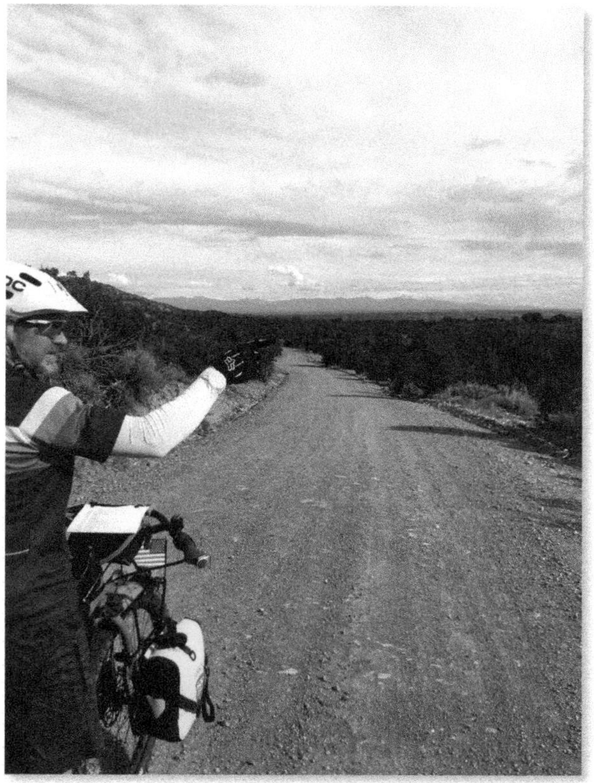

While riding, we see the typical sights we have come to know along the rural roads of the US: mobile homes, a couple of dogs, forlorn trampolines, and various car parts and unused gadgets. We know what's ahead of us with each stroke of the pedal—a steady climb of 4,000 feet from Abiquiu to our primitive campsite outside, according to the maps. Each peak we conquer only presents us with another. The motivation to keep moving slowly dissipates, until it's as thin as the air we are breathing.

The beauty of the hills and mountains helps us mentally. The higher we climb, the more spectacular the views. With hill climbs come inevitable valleys. Each time we dip into a valley, we enter a flood zone. Some of them are really scary, because it's obvious that the mud and runoff is very recent. Thankfully, when the rain starts to come down on us, we find ourselves at an elevation that is out of the flood zone.

Nonetheless, at 4:00 p.m. we are still climbing. The sun has come out, and the rain has stopped. We bike for another hour. At 5:00 p.m. we are struggling to keep moving. My final spin of the day ticks my odometer to exactly the 2900-mile mark—650 miles of training and 2,250 on the trail—which leaves us only 500 miles to go. This is a little boost of accomplishment and another reason to keep pushing.

The area around us seems to be blanketed with moss, making the ground seem soft and desirable to lie on, so we decide to stop and camp. We don't know where the next valley is, and staying high is the safe thing to do. Once camp is pitched, John and I find the softest patch of moss and just lie down, looking up at the blue sky, enjoying the sights, sounds, and smells.

As I have mentioned before, in primitive camping, there are no services—no tables, no toilets, and no water. Because there is no water access, we decide it's best not to have a campfire because we don't have enough drinking water to make sure the fire is put out completely. Without fire, dinner is a boiled Rice-a-Roni packet on our stove and some leftover potatoes from the restaurant in Abiquiu.

We are at 10,000 feet in elevation, and today's journey was both mentally and physically tough. We covered only 31 miles because of the steep hills and held a slow pace of 5.1 miles per hour.

The coyotes howl through the night, and at times it feels like they are circling us. Paranoia and thin air can fog the mind. They probably never got that close during the night, but this campsite is truly remote—and the lack of humans does make room for some curious predators.

Ending day stats:

Start 8:40 a.m. Finish 4:20 p.m.
8 hours and 40 minutes
31.44 miles

GDMBR Day 40
August 30, Tuesday

Weather—Overcast, rain, hail, sun
A primitive campsite to Cuba, NM

John's Notes: Two days ago, we set our goal of reaching Cuba, with full services. Waking up this morning we know this is doable.

No sign of civilization—anywhere. A wild experience.

The morning dew is so heavy that the tent feels like it rained all night. Rolling it up is like rolling up a wet towel, and we don't want to spend a ton of time trying to dry it out. We have many miles to cover today, and we get an early start to take advantage of the currently clear sky.

I expected the New Mexico section to look more like the terrain in Abiquiu—flat vistas, scenic rock formations, and a desert-like topography. Instead, we are constantly climbing while surrounded by large evergreen trees and breathing thin air. It smells like fresh rain, tinged with the scent of pine needles. The smell brings back fond childhood memories of camping at Mammoth Mountain, California.

We continue to climb . . .

As the temperature drops quickly, the rain begins. We continue to climb, so it's really no surprise when we come across snow on the ground. As we reach the summit and start our downhill ride, the rain continues. I have not been this wet or this muddy so far on the journey. We have this saying at home, "It's a great day biking when you are muddy or bloody." I try to embrace my own mantra, but find myself cold, hungry, and angry at the weather.

The final 10 miles to Cuba prove to be easy—all downhill and on a paved road. Our descent leads us into a valley, and then the sun comes out causing a 30-degree temperature swing. As we look back and see the elevation behind us, we feel a great sense of accomplishment.

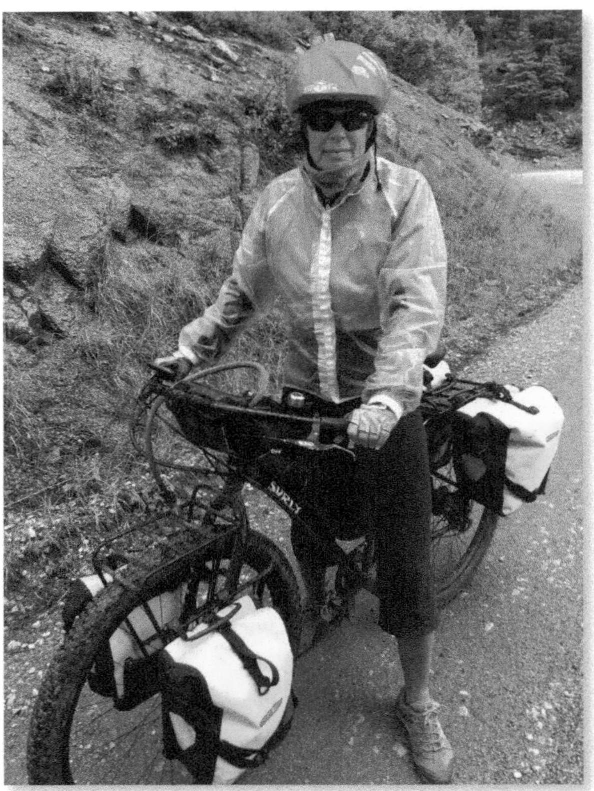

When we reach Cuba we find a small town like the many others we've visited during our ride. It is clear to us that this town's glory days—its booming years—are long gone. Today's Cuba is a tired shadow of its glory days. The place has been left behind. There is, however, a motel still in business, and more importantly, they have a room available for us.

Hoping for GDMBR riders like us, the hotel has a hose and a grassy area where John rinses off our bikes and bodies. We unpack our tent and drape it over the fence to let it dry out in the hot sun. It's hard to believe that we started our morning with the coyotes in the mountains of New Mexico and ended our day in the sweltering heat of the desert.

I find a laundromat where we can run a load of laundry. As we park our bikes in front, my sunglasses fall off and I run them over, crushing them, not fixable. All this way and no complaints about my sunglasses—by the way, I have been wearing them 12 hours a day, and they never hurt my head or my nose. Across the street is a liquor store, where for the first time on the trail, I discover Sutter Home wine minis—in plastic bottles, so I can take them with me on the trail. This is the best discovery! I can't help but wonder if things would have been different had I found them sooner—say back in Banff.

I open one of these little bottles and sip as John and I face our next decision: Do we bike through mud and rain tomorrow, knowing we may very well encounter some flooding? Or do we ride the 125 miles on the highway—absent of campsites, necessitating completing all 125 miles in one day?

Ending day stats:

Start 8:00 a.m. Finish 4:00 p.m.
8 hours
55.71 miles

GDMBR Day 41
August 31, Wednesday

Weather—Sun, hot
Cuba to Grants, NM

John's Notes: This is one of the most difficult decisions we have to make on this journey. After talking about it all night with Carrie, we came to the conclusion that our safety was in jeopardy. That brought clarity to me, making it apparent that we needed a way to get to Grants without having to choose between riding in the monsoon rain area where we might get stuck or having nowhere to safely sleep for the night, which would cause us to bike 125 miles in one day. We needed a third option.

One big adventure after another.

We wake up early and decide it's not safe enough to bike the alternative route—125 miles of highway. Since the main route is unbikeable at this time due to the monsoon rains, we opt for catching a ride. Going from the polar opposites of not seeing a human for the past 48 hours to modern, bustling, noisy life—even in quiet Cuba—overwhelms me.

I call Michelle and ask for her help. We need to find a way to get from Cuba to Grants. She agrees that we are making the right decision. Nate, her boyfriend, has found a guy on Craigslist who can pick us up first thing—tomorrow. However, we aren't feeling that patient, so we decide to pack up and check out of the hotel. We hope that we can secure a ride and not hang out in Cuba for a day.

We start our search at the Conoco gas station directly next to our hotel. I go inside and ask the girl at the counter how she would go about hitching a ride to Grants. Meanwhile, John is talking to people fueling up, and he immediately finds us a ride with two really nice men—they are headed to Albuquerque, halfway to Grants.

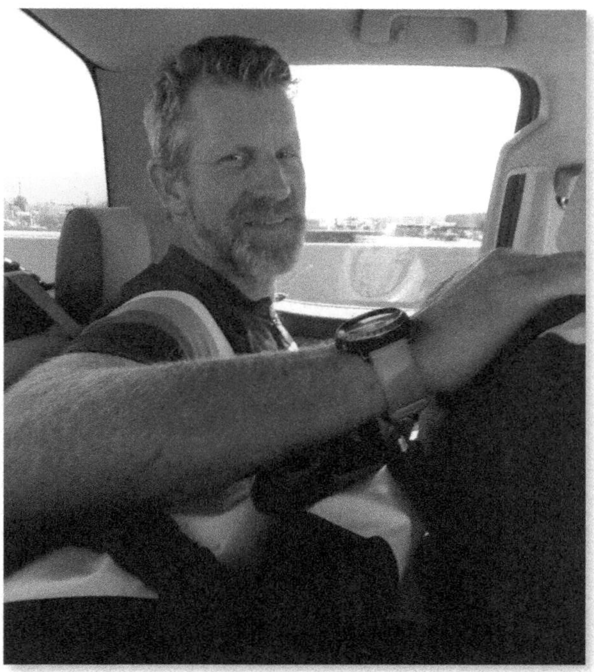

It doesn't take long to get our bikes packed up in their truck. Before we know it we're on the road to Albuquerque. We have a lively conversation with the two men, Mario and Billy. Mario is a musician and has played thousands of gigs. He is the lead singer in a small band based in Farmington, and plays many instruments—guitar, drums, piano. Billy is a jokester. He reminds us of John's friend, also named Billy, who is equally as funny.

Mario and Billy have known each other since birth. During the drive, they point out where their mothers and grandmothers were born, and tell us the names of the mountains in the distance, sharing the best ice-caving spots to come back to visit. Best yet, they are Broncos fans, so there is much to talk about as the season is just getting started!

Unfortunately, the ride ends too soon. Albuquerque is only 70 miles from Cuba, which is a pretty quick journey by car. They drop us off close to the airport so we can rent a car and drive to Grants. We say bittersweet goodbyes to our new friends, and talk about going to one of Mario's gigs sometime in the future.

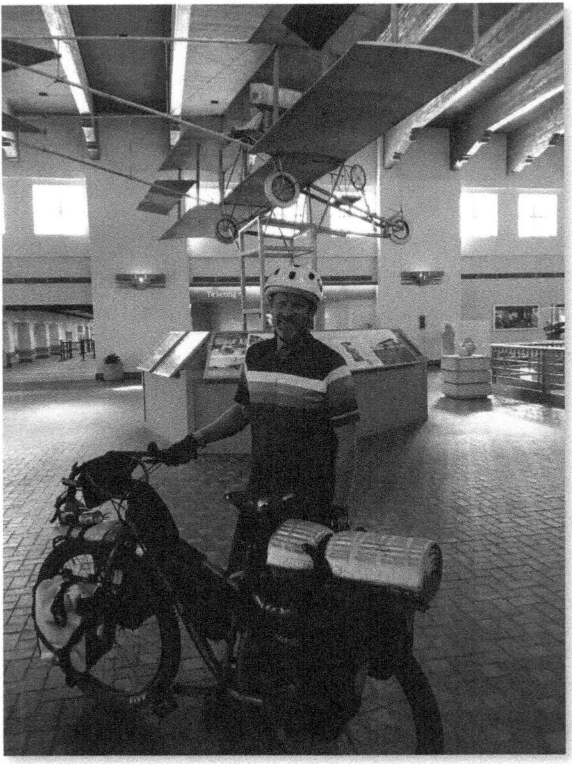

We bike to the airport and soon find ourselves "in" the airport. Albuquerque's airport is interesting, to say the least; part of it is outside and part of it is inside. We can feel the strange looks as we walk our bikes through. A policeman approaches us and asks, "Can I help you? You look a little lost." We explain our situation, telling him we're looking for the rental car counters. He tells us that they are located off-site.

We bike "out" of the airport and down to the car rental center. When we get there, we are told by every rental car company that we cannot drop the car in Grants, so no one will rent us a car. I am again paralyzed by the entire ordeal, and I just can't think straight. Maybe it's because we have been in the wilderness so long that modern conveniences seem foreign.

I tell John I will come up with a solution, and not knowing what to do, I call Michelle again. This time she recommends we try to find an Uber XL to Grants, as they should have enough room in their car for our bikes, our panniers, and us.

I order the Uber and our driver arrives in a Honda Pilot. This just might work out after all. John disassembles the bikes and we help pack the car. It is full to capacity, and soon we are on our way to Grants where we can get back on the trail. I call the Holiday Inn Express in Grants from the car, and we are able to get a room for the night.

What a day, what an adventure, what a relief.

Ending day stats:

Two car rides, trip through airport

Zero biked miles (We're not counting miles to and from the airport.)

GDMBR Day 41–do over
September 1, Thursday

Weather—Sun, overcast, rain
Grants to Pie Town, NM

John's Notes: With no biking yesterday, we feel we can push a little harder, shooting for Pie Town with services as our goal. Pie Town is famous on the GDMBR, as it is clearly marked on all the maps.

We have been dreaming of Pie since we left Banff, Canada.

We get up extra early today because we have another big day ahead of us. Unfortunately, the day does not start off the way we would like it to. On our way out of the hotel, we turn left instead of right, and eventually hit a dead end. Not a big deal, we just need to turn around and head the right way. However, John notices that his cyclometer is no longer working, so we turn around. We are still in town, so we stop at a Walgreens and buy a new battery. Unfortunately, changing out the battery does not fix his cyclometer. So, after 41 days of following John's turn-by-turn directions, we are suddenly without the cyclometer to confirm each turn at each mile.

I am getting anxious about the time we are spending and let John know. "We have to get going," I say, trying not to increase the pressure we both already feel.

John pulls out the green Adventure Cycling Association (ACA) maps to review our distance for the day, including how many turns it will take to get to our destination. We literally have only one turn and it is clearly marked—Pie Town.

We finally get started on the trail—the famous Route 66. The road is flat and paved, the sky is clear, and the sun is shining. By noon we have already biked 50 miles. We stop where we can find a small shaded spot on the side of the dirt road. Only 25 miles to go until Pie Town—the countdown starts.

After lunch, we are reminded that there are no easy days on the GDMBR. The skies cloud over and it begins to rain. The hills get steeper and longer, and Pie Town seems so far away. A few miles outside of Pie Town, we run into a backpacker whose trail name is Glider. He has just spent four days at the Toaster House, a hostel in Pie Town. We are planning to stay there tonight. He tells us good things about the hostel and I get excited, as I have never stayed in a hostel before.

John and I are beyond excited to eat dinner at the Pie Town Cafe and want to make sure we get there before it closes. As we summit the last hill and roll up to the cafe, we find it's closed.

WTF? All these miles to Pie Town and the cafe is closed?! Pissed off comes to mind.

Thankfully, the Pie-O-Neer is open. Because of the afternoon's pouring rain, we are soaking wet and want to change into dry clothes before entering the cafe. There isn't enough time to bike to the Toaster House, clean up, and make it back to the Pie-O-Neer for dinner. So we do our best to dry off before entering the restaurant.

As usual, we enter the restaurant completely famished. We end up drinking four Sprites each, sharing a small pie before dinner, and then eating a full dinner. A few locals at the cafe are talking about the annual Pie Festival that is coming up for Labor Day weekend. One woman has already baked 650 pies. Her husband, clearly a rancher, is carrying his gun in the back of his pants—not a sight we see too often where we live.

The pies are small in size, so I purchase a couple extra for tomorrow's breakfast and lunch. It is pouring rain again. So after dinner we have to put our wet rain gear back on before we cycle to the Toaster House. We are happy to find a room for the night—delighted we don't have to camp in the rain and blessed to have a dry room, a warm shower, and a washing machine. This place is eclectic, to say the least. It is a modest home, decorated with toasters on the outside, and pictures, gear, and living essentials on the inside. (You can Google it and check out all the posted photos.)

Everyone is welcome at the Toaster House, and rooms are assigned on a first- come, first-served basis. Pie Town is another spot where the GDMBR and the Continental Divide Trail (CDT) intersect. Both bikers and hikers have stayed at this fairly famous house. Payment is what you can afford, and people stock the kitchen with an array of items—peanut butter and jelly, coffee, tea, and there was even a frozen pizza in the freezer. When the rain stops, we sit on the porch on old car seats while we chat with another hiker. His trail name—a common facet of the Continental

Divide Trail and other major hiking routes—is Phantom.

Phantom is a character from London and is trying to be the first Continental Divide Trail hiker in 2016 to hike from north to south. He tells us, "My nemesis, a young chap with the trail name Mammoth, is lurking close behind me." Mammoth is half the age of Phantom and can walk 50 miles a day. Phantom can hike only 30 miles a day. He cracks us up by telling us how he is staying ahead of Mammoth—by using GPS.

We enjoy the comfort of the house, the conversation with Phantom, and the eclectic decor outside. There is a wall of hanging shoes left by hundreds of people before us, and I am sure there will be more hung in the future. We know we are close to finishing, but we don't know how easy or hard these final days are about to become.

Ending day stats:
Start 7:10 a.m. Finish 4:00 p.m.
8 hours and 50 minutes
72.74 miles

GDMBR Day 42
September 2, Friday

Start of the three-day weekend
Weather—Sun
Pie Town to Collins Park, NM

John's Notes: The beginning of the three-day weekend, hunting season, and rain all pose threats on our ability to find campsites. There are no services for the next couple of days. We have to stock up on food and water, which adds a lot of weight to our already heavy bikes. We will have to push hard. Primitive campsite is where we will sleep tonight.

Trust in people. They just might surprise you.

John and I start our morning by sharing leftover pie. Wouldn't it be nice if every day could start and end in Pie Town! Right off the bat, there is a hill climb. Fields of wildflowers are in full bloom on both sides of the route; it's really quite beautiful. The flowers are so full and lush because the monsoon rains are in season, though this has an adverse impact on the road—icky, sticky mud. We can't even get our tires to spin through it. John is worried that we will continue to encounter this mud for the next few days, which would certainly make the trip that much harder.

After an hour of starting and stopping to clear the mud out of our tires with a stick from the side of the road, we make it out of the mud zone. Now we are just climbing. John and I continue to take note of the fact that the New Mexico topography is not what we expected. The forests are dense and the roads are steep and rocky—and the muddiest we've encountered on the entire trip.

Furthermore, water is an issue during this part of the route. Per the maps and the McCoy book, it will be tough to find water for the next four days. John and I pack enough in our panniers to last us two days and plan to refill at the places marked. However, each time we come across a spot where there is supposed to be water, we end up disappointed when we discover it is dry as dust.

John starts to worry.

Fortunately, it's Labor Day weekend, which means that there should be campers on the backcountry routes with us, and we are hopeful that some of them will have enough water to share. I know that if we get in a real pinch, I can always beg. The trail is remote, filled with green grass and blooming wildflowers. Birds are flying around us and occasionally we see a herd of cattle.

Around 5:00 p.m. we get passed by a truck filled with a family and pulling a camper. Shortly after they pass us we come across them stopped on the side of the road making a phone call. I stop at their window to make sure everything is okay; they say it is. We ride down the road for a mile or so before they pass us again and stop just ahead of us. John and I ride up to the window and see what's going on. The wife apologizes to us for stopping their truck and camper in front of us and taking up the road earlier when they were making their phone call. They ask us what we are doing, and we tell them that we've biked from Banff, Canada, to this point, and that we only have a few more days before we reach our final destination in Antelope Wells, Mexico—the end of our Great Divide Mountain Bike Route journey. They are completely blown away. I ask them if they know where we can find some water. The husband immediately says, "We have a ton of water, would you like some?" I am incredibly grateful for the offer, and without hesitation respond, "Yes, please!"

He hops out of his truck and helps us fill our water bottles and our extra water holders. They have just set us up with water for the next two days, and a huge sense of relief washes over us. After thanking them over and over for their generosity, they head on their way, and John and I continue our steady push to tonight's campsite. Though the raindrops come and go, we are able to make great time and speed along on a fairly flat route. The fields of sunflowers are at their peak, making the ride all the more beautiful. We cross the Continental Divide three times today, but it is not as dramatic as our crossings were in Colorado.

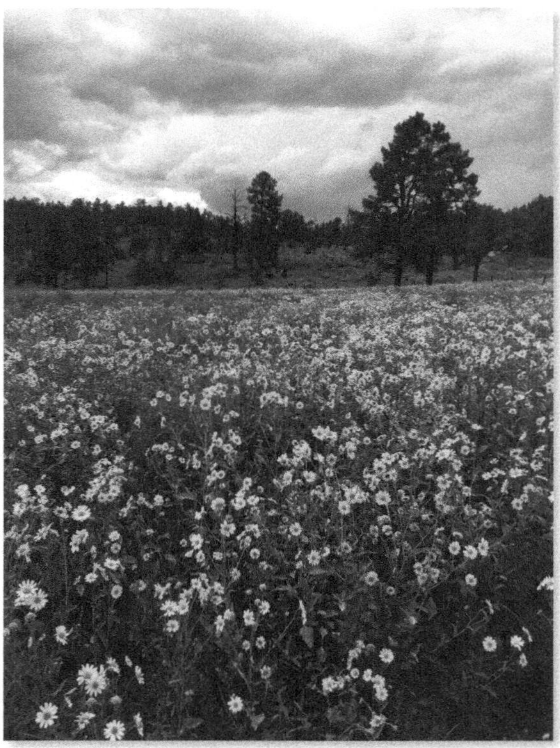

John and I start to talk about where we should camp for the night. Since the route is so flat, and our pace is much faster than normal, we continue biking. Our legs feel strong, and the farther we get today, the easier tomorrow will be.

Around 5:45 p.m. we pass a hunter in full gear—his face painted—riding a four-wheeler. As we pass him he stops and asks, "Where the hell are you going?" We tell him about our trip and that we are starting to look for a campsite, but we are not really in a hurry to find one. He introduces himself as Irv from Arvada, Colorado. What are the chances of our running into a Colorado hunter while in the wilderness of New Mexico? After we talk for a few more minutes, Irv invites us to come to his campsite and camp with him for the night. He gestures nonchalantly toward the horizon, telling us he's "about five miles that way." "That way" is the same direction we're headed.

A vibrant rainbow appears as we bike into Irv's campsite, and I yell, "Irv, we're here!" He is so excited, telling us he's glad we found him, and man, are we glad too. His campsite has all the bells and whistles: cases of water, several coolers full of food, a sink to wash your hands with a foot pump that pumps water through the faucet, and even a dining table with chairs. This is pure camping luxury. He even has a potty chair, which he offers to share with us. It is a metal chair that has a toilet seat attached, and a hole cut in the middle. "Just dig a hole, do your business, cover up the waste with dirt, and you are good to go," Irv tells us.

After setting up our tent and changing out of our wet and sweaty clothes, we join Irv for dinner and drinks. Irv has been out in the woods for a week and is prepared to stay two more weeks to hunt. He's a retired police officer who served on the Albuquerque Police Department. After retiring, he and his girlfriend moved to Colorado, where she was relocated for work.

I enjoy a glass of wine with Irv. He offers us chips and salsa and we share stories with one another until the night comes to a close. John and I head to bed feeling blessed to have found water and to have met Irv. Knowing this journey will soon end, we find ourselves feeling more and more thankful for the moments like these on the trail, and that kind people like the family and Irv are still in the world, making it a better place.

Ending day stats:

Start 7:45 a.m. Finish 6:15 p.m.
10 hours and 30 minutes
72.02 miles

GDMBR Day 43
September 3, Saturday

Weather—Rain, sun
Collins Park to Black Canyon Campground, NM

John's Notes: The thought of finishing the GDMBR is becoming more real for us, but we are not there yet. We have our two-day goal set on reaching Silver City, about 110 miles away. We are fully loaded with water thanks to Irv, giving us the boost of confidence we need.

> *Every act of kindness we experience on the trail comes from random people. We believe most people are good, and this bike ride across America proves to us how right we are.*

It pours rain most of the night. Because John covered our tent with the blue tarp, the rain did not penetrate the tent. We know it will make today's bike ride even harder. The New Mexico mud is famous on the GDMBR for being able to stop you in your tracks. When we get up, Irv has been long gone; we heard him leave camp at 4:00 a.m. He is elk hunting with a bow and arrow. The tag he has is for a dedicated spot about 14 miles from camp.

John and I linger at the campsite in the morning, enjoying Irv's luxuries and filling up our water reserves. The road in the beginning is in much better condition than expected. There are sunflowers and beautiful ranches breaching the horizon, with the sunlight casting a beautiful glow behind them. The rock formations are tall and grand, the sky is deep blue, and the birds are out flying around us singing and eating bugs.

Then, we hit the mud . . .

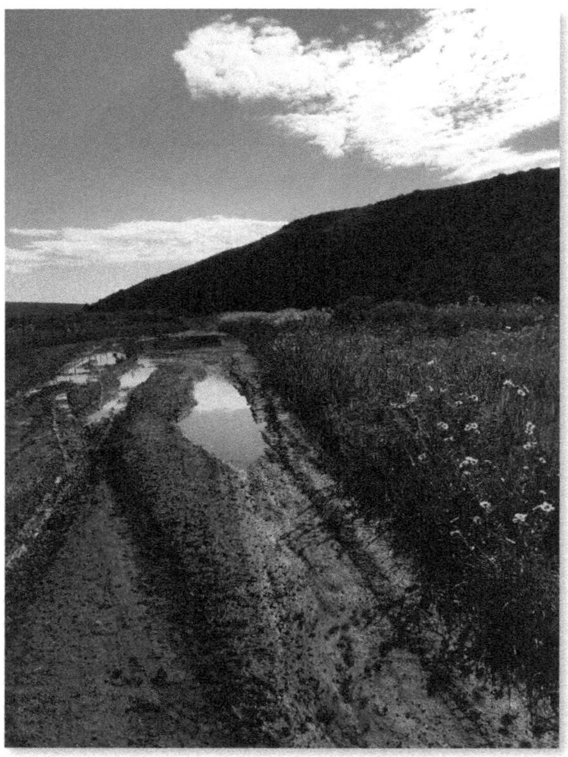

The road is filled from side to side with dense mud and deep water puddles. The birds seem incredibly happy to play in the water and mud, but we are not. This is exactly what we had been reading about, but we had yet to experience it to its fullest. John and I had even read that some people abandon their bikes because it can be so bad, opting instead to hike out of the forest and return to their bikes later. Luckily it isn't that bad for us. However, we still have to stop every 10 minutes or so to scrape the mud away from the tires, as they won't rotate. Our goal is to bike around 50 miles today. It's going to be challenging to make that goal, though, especially at our current pace. It's only 9:00 a.m., and we have not logged many miles at all.

After spending more than three hours in the mud zone for most of the morning, we enter the Gila National Forest and start climbing. It feels as if we are leaving the mud zone behind us as we gain elevation. Our map indicates that we're approaching a "workstation," and that there should be water. It's nearly lunchtime—definitely time for a break. To be clear, we have enough water to make it to our next stop, but it would be nice to refill what we've consumed.

The weather has gone from pleasant and cool to hot and stifling. John and I find some shade where we can eat our lunch, and I bring out a bean-and-cheese burrito that has seen better days—especially since we bought it back in Grants, three days ago! We do find a pump station with plenty of water. The desire to bathe in the water overcomes us both; it's hot outside and it's been a day and a half since we've showered. While we feel like getting wet, we find the sunny spot to be the perfect place to unroll our tent and let it dry out.

Several hunters stop at the station for water. They see our bikes and are very curious about our mode of travel. We strike up conversations with all who come to the pump. One set of hunters can't help but share their morning, which included a hot shower, a big hot breakfast, and a truck they can use to drive wherever they want in quick fashion. Our morning consisted of hot tea, oatmeal, a stale bagel, and stepping back into our dirty clothes. When comparing campsite stories, the hunters claim their camp is primitive because they don't have TV like some of the other hunters. After hearing how we've been camping—no running water, no toilet, limited access to food—they think about their camp a little differently.

On our way out of the workstation, I wave goodbye to this set of hunters, who are staying for a bit more water. They stop us and hand us a couple of granola bars. The hunter who gives them to me says, "It's not much, but you might need the food more than we do."

The kindness people have shown us on our journey is something I won't ever forget. When I return to normal life, I hope to remember to share small random acts of kindness to others and not get lost in the fray of everyday life. I know how much these acts have meant to us.

After leaving our lunch spot at the workstation, the day continues to get harder and harder. Long uphill treks are interrupted only by short downhill respites before more long uphill treks. The heat is beating down with force. There is not much shade. When we come across a small lake with a nice flowing stream, we gladly stop for a quick dip. We don't have time to take off all our clothes and really enjoy the water, but it feels nice to put our feet and legs in the cool water.

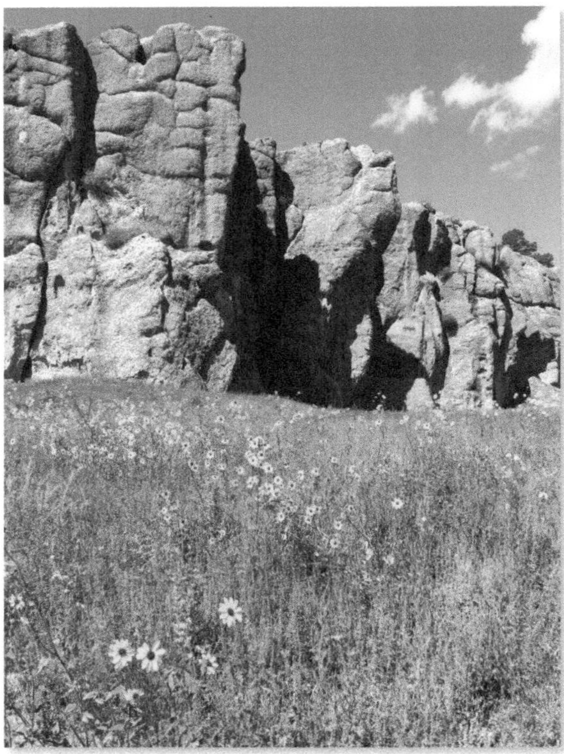

Shortly after the lake, some hunters stop by and offer us a lift in their pickup truck. I have to be honest, this is very tempting. We decline because we want to prove to ourselves that we can do this.

Nonetheless, by 4:00 p.m. I am getting discouraged. I know how far we have left to go, and the elevation gains on the map are revealing more steady uphill climbs. We stop often to rest our legs, drink water, and eat a snack. Even though these stops are often the rest and fuel we need to keep going, it doesn't change the fact that the miles and time continue to tick slowly and that camp is a distant dream at this point.

We keep climbing and climbing and climbing, and at some point the road changes to washboard and loose rock. I am thinking this is Saturday, just the beginning of what should feel like a luxurious three-day weekend, instead feels like a torturous weekday. It's not fun! I turn to John and tell him that this is the worst three-day weekend of my life. I am mentally and physically done, and I take it out on him—which I totally regret. Limited access to food, water, and toilets while relentlessly pushing my body to its breaking point is *not* my idea of a holiday weekend.

By 6:00 p.m. we have finally reached the top of the final summit, and we have a steep downhill remaining. But the ride to camp takes a little bit longer than expected because of the loose gravel and steep cliff edge. Having to pump the brakes so hard for so long causes my fingers to start going numb. We finally reach the campsite, a beautiful spot right on a river. The first site we see is available, and we park our bikes immediately. There's a picnic table, a portable toilet, and a fire pit, plenty of dead wood around for us to gather and have a nice campfire. One of the luxuries of having a campsite on the water is that we can always build a fire, since we don't have to worry about putting it out with our drinking water. As darkness falls, we listen to the crackling of the fire and the hiss of embers. We can hear folks at the other campsites around us laughing. Everyone is having a good time, and the vibe rubs off on us too. I regret my meltdown of earlier, and am so grateful we have each other on this journey.

We go to bed knowing that we have only three days left—we have finally started the countdown. We know the last three days will be difficult, but we are so close to finishing, and now each of us can buckle down mentally and finish strong.

Ending day stats:

Start 8:35 a.m. Finish 6:15 p.m.
9 hours and 40 minutes
53.42 miles

GDMBR Day 44
September 4, Sunday

End of week seven
Weather—Sun, hot
Black Canyon Campground to Silver City, NM

John's Notes: We've got only 60 miles to Silver City where we can get full services—just the motivation we need to get through another day. The map shows some steep climbs, with a nice long downhill at the end of the day.

The end of a long trail approaches.

We wake up in the morning just as the sun is starting to come out, amped to get the journey started and tick off another day. We're excited to be headed to a city that has plenty of food and water. According to the maps, this is going to be our final day of hill climbing. In other words, this will be our last hard-ass day on the entire journey. The light at the end of the tunnel is clear as day.

John asks me, "Was this trip worth it? Were your comments yesterday afternoon harsh just because of the conditions of the ride?"

I nod, feeling penitent, and apologize again for having been so short with him. Then we turn our talk to the good parts of the trip. We conclude with dissecting how—and why—yesterday had been so incredibly hard. We're both happy and relieved to put it behind us. Silver City, here we come!

Since we are in the backcountry with very little traffic and because the day is already very hot, John decides to take off his bike shorts and ride only with the padded compression underwear. As he takes off his shorts I immediately burst out laughing. His bike shorts have rotted, and there is a huge hole in the ass of his shorts where the seam has split. We have a good laugh, and he puts his shorts back on.

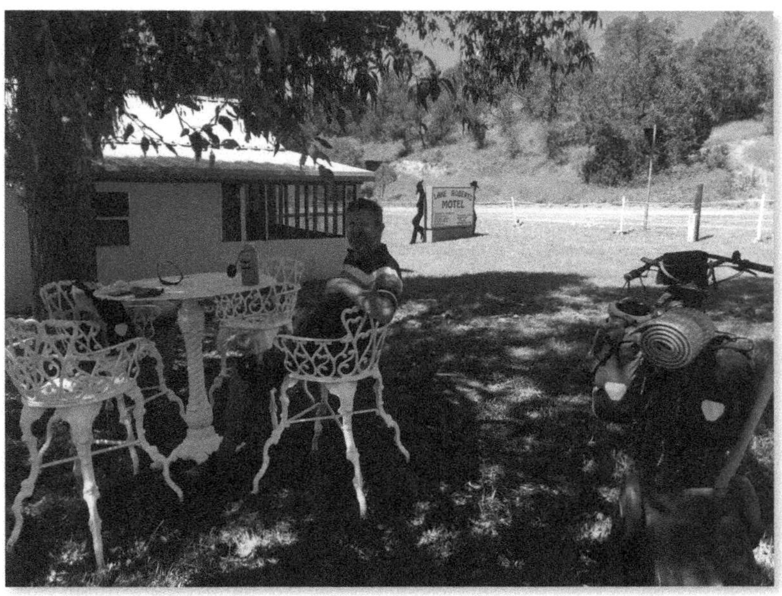

We reach the top of the first summit, and we're pretty excited to have downhill for the rest of the way. That's what our map indicates at least, but we soon discover that this is not the case. It seems like we stay up high in elevation for most of the day. The vistas are beautiful, and we can feel that the cars next to us on the small two-lane back roads are mainly out enjoying the beauty of the surrounding nature. We climb hills all day. There are certainly some long downhills, and that helps us get through some of the tougher climbs. The route is mostly on paved road, so we are able to tick off the miles and not get too jolted.

In one of the valleys near Lake Roberts where we stop for lunch, we're surrounded by sunflowers that are taller than John. They are thick and tall on each side of the road; their beauty is mesmerizing. The downhill into Lake Roberts is a welcome reprieve from the hills we've been climbing all morning. We can see hundreds of people playing and splashing around in the lake, enjoying the cool water on such a hot day. We are just excited to get to the cafe and eat, but when we arrive at Lake Roberts there is no cafe to be found.

So John and I stop at the general store in a hotel along the route, where we buy a full bag of ice, canned veggies, canned peaches, two large Gatorades, a bag of chips, and Oreos for dessert. The owners allow us to sit on their shaded lawn where we can rest and enjoy lunch. John is able to get the entire bag of ice into our water bladders, our red water container, and our extra water bag. On a hot day, cold water is a necessity, and we now have cold water all the way to Silver City.

Shortly after leaving Lake Roberts, we go back to climbing. However, there is one thing different about this hill—it will be the last hill we climb for the rest of the trip! Still, we climb for three and a half hours after leaving our lunch spot. The last hill of the journey is definitely a doozy.

On the final leg of the route to Silver City we pass through Pinos Altos, a cute town where the old opera house and saloon still stand. From here, it's all downhill into Silver City, baby! Twenty miles of downhill, and then we'll be at our hotel where we can take a hot shower, do laundry, and buy fresh food!

As we enter Silver City, I finally get cell service. After days, I am beyond thrilled to be connected. The first thing I have to do is secure a hotel close to the route, which I'm able to find at a Holiday Inn Express. As we focus in on my Google maps to find our way to the hotel, we come upon a grocery store on the right and immediately pull in to restock. For the past several days we've been camping and relying on—suffering through—processed food. My body is ready to rebel. When I reach the produce department, I fill my basket with two of everything—fresh peaches, tomatoes, avocados—and then move on to fresh bagels and tortillas for our final two days on the GDMBR.

As John loads up the panniers with all this new food, I get a FaceTime call from Michelle. She and Nate are in New Hampshire at her grandparents' house for Labor Day weekend and to celebrate Nate's birthday.

Then our daughter tells us her news: Nate has proposed to her, out on a rock in the middle of the lake.

That's right: In the parking lot of a grocery store in Silver City, New Mexico, we find out that our only daughter is getting married. Of course we're ecstatic; we all love Nate, and feel beyond blessed that our daughter is marrying such a great guy. As I watch John gently nudge the new peaches into my pannier, I feel heady with joy, relief, and awe. In all our planning for this exhilarating and excruciating bike ride across North America, I never imagined it would end like this. What a journey!

John and I get to the hotel, devour some fresh food, and celebrate Nate and Michelle's engagement. The local pizza joint delivers a large veggie pizza and we eat the whole thing. Real food, after days in the wilderness, is such a treat.

John's parents are preparing to pick us up in two days. Having biked across the country themselves several years back, they know that we will be filled with stories of adventure, and they don't want to miss out on any of them. We confirm with them on the phone where we should meet in Antelope Wells.

Then John and I sit down to prepare for the final two days of the trip. We are praying that the monsoon rains don't return and that we make it safely to Hachita tomorrow—and then to Antelope Wells, which is on the Mexican border. With just 125 miles to go, we are starting to realize just how close we are to the end.

Ending day stats:

Start 7:35 a.m. Finish 4:00 p.m.
8 hours and 25 minutes
60.32 miles

GDMBR Day 45
September 5, Monday

Weather—Sun, over 90 degrees
Silver City to Hachita, NM

John's Notes: There is just one more overnight stop before the end of the journey. Our safety is my biggest concern, as Hachita, New Mexico, is just 40 miles from the Mexican border. We only have our bikes and one can of bear spray to protect us, and this causes me to worry. We've heard the area is often frequented by human smugglers, and we don't want to find ourselves in the wrong place at the wrong time. I'm afraid of the unknown—but if we're going to finish this thing, we've got to keep riding.

With our daughter engaged, nothing can stop us from smiling.

We wake up extra early this morning, probably from the sheer anticipation of being so close to the end. However, we have a long 81-mile bike ride to Hachita—a ride we won't finish if the monsoon rains return.

The ride starts out on the highway for the first 20 miles. Getting here early allows us to miss much of the traffic, thus making the ride all the more pleasant. One of the sights we're treated to while riding on the highway is a driveway decorated with toilets all the way from the road to the house. This makes us laugh, because toilets have been somewhat of a rarity for us on the trip; to see so many that aren't actually being used is quite funny. As we turn off the highway and onto a red sand road, the evidence of flash floods is clear. We are worried that the rains could come at any time while we're biking though this desert valley. Urgency is our mantra of the morning, and we're making great time, ticking through miles in this flash-flood area.

At 10:30 we stop for our morning snack. We have been in the saddle for three hours and my legs need a break. The desert beauty displays wild flowers and bugs that I have never seen before. Unfortunately, there is nowhere to sit and no shade. The heat is steadily creeping higher, and we know that we'll soon be at the peak heat of the day. I ask John, "Has it sunk in yet, that thirty-six hours from now we will be done with the route?"

He smiles.

"What kind of emotion," I ask, "do you think we'll feel when we finish?"

He says he's not sure.

Thinking about my question, all I know for sure is that it has been a wild ride, accomplishing such a grueling feat. We get back on our bikes and pedal on.

By noon we reach Interstate 10—we've already biked 51 miles. When we reach a trading post just off the interstate, we're warmly greeted by the women behind the counters. They immediately tell us where the bathrooms are and that all GDMBR riders are welcome. While buying several cold drinks, ice, and water, we ask about the safety of camping in Hachita. To our surprise, the lady at the counter tells us that she is friends with the man who runs the community center, and that they often open it up to riders and hikers, offering them a safe place to stay. She gives us his number. Out on the trading post porch I quickly give him a call.

Jeffrey answers after a few rings. He tells us that he'd be happy to open the community center for us, and that we can help ourselves to the full kitchen of snacks as well. In other words, make ourselves at home. John looks visibly relieved after I give him the good news, and he goes back to thank the ladies who gave us Jeffrey's phone number.

When he comes back out of the store, he's crying. I didn't understand just how worried he was for my safety during this section of the route until right now. I give him a hug. Our love for each other has been the deepest I have ever experienced in the 25 years we've been married. We can't live without each other, and this ride, this journey, has brought us even closer together.

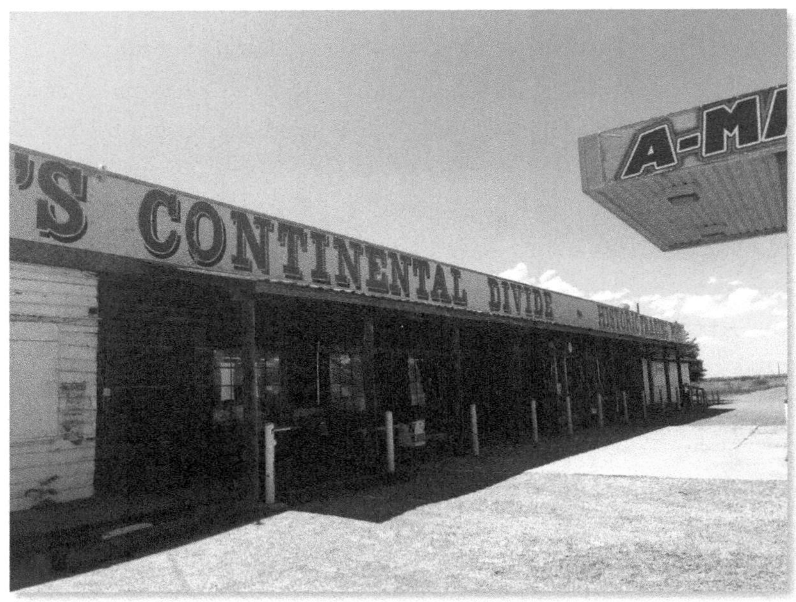

We stay at the trading post for another hour and a half before getting back on the route. The shade is hard to leave, and we have only 30 flat miles left for the day—easy. But those 30 miles are brutal in the relentless sun. There are no clouds, no shade, and the heat beats down fiercely.

When we reach Hachita, we find the community center doors are unlocked for us. We quickly get out of our hot and stinky clothes and unpack our food so we can put it in the refrigerator. We are the only guests at the community center tonight; it's nice to have it to ourselves. John finds a hose in the back of the building and a newly installed water spigot in the front. We grab our hotel soap, hop into bathing suits, and take a shower right on Main Street.

From the plaque on the wall we learn that Hachita has a small-town history like many other small towns—boom to bust; from trains to trucks to coal mining. There are currently fewer than 40 people still living in Hachita.

The evening brings a beautiful sunset, followed by a lightning storm. We take some chairs outside to watch the storm. While it rains hard on 4th Street on the west side of the building, it stays bone dry on 3rd Street, the east side of the building.

While the dark clouds slowly creep in—the only light still alive flashes for split seconds, cracking the night open momentarily and then fading into black—we are suddenly struck by the fact that this is officially our last night on the journey. In 24 hours from now, John and I will be finishers of the Great Divide Mountain Bike Route.

As we lie down in our sleeping bags on the stage in the community center, the flies buzz around and the crickets chirp. I pull up the photos on my phone and we look back and talk about different parts of the trail, both good and bad. The memories will be forever with us to relive and revisit—hopefully often and fondly as time passes.

Ending day stats:

Start 7:15 a.m. Finish 4:10 p.m.
8 hours and 55 minutes
81.03 miles

GDMBR Day 46
September 6, Tuesday

Weather—Overcast, rain, cool
Hachita to Antelope Wells, NM

John's Notes: The goal for the end is clear, just 45 miles to Antelope Wells, a place we have talked about from the beginning. The end is always bittersweet; both of us are mentally and physically ready to finish.

Emotional day for the two of us.

We wake up early, raring to go. This is the last morning we will pack up our sleeping bags, secure our panniers to our bikes, and step into our dirty biking clothes. We are ready to finish!

The weather is overcast this morning, which is such a blessing because it's actually cool instead of brutally hot. The ride to the border features expansive mountains on each side, so we are able to enjoy a scenic final ride to Antelope Wells.

Five miles into the ride, emotions take over and I start to cry. The emotion of completing this journey is profound—and unlike anything I have ever accomplished before. I try to hold back the tears, as I haven't cried on this trip. Then I think: Why should I hold back my tears? I can cry if I want to.

John has been my rock the entire ride, encouraging me, motivating me, and supporting me. I pull off the road so I can hug him and tell him how much I love him—and when he gets off his bike, he is crying, too. We are totally in sync with each other on this journey, and the emotions of finishing it together touch us both at the same time.

While he's holding me in his arms, I can't help it and I start to sob. I tell him how grateful I am that he encouraged me to take this trip with him and that he dared me to finish what is touted as one of the toughest bike routes in all of North America.

When the embrace ends and the tears stop rolling, we talk about the future—about other trips and adventures. This is not the end; it is just another beginning. Nonetheless, we still need to finish what we set out to accomplish: to become Great Divide Mountain Bike Route FINISHERS.

With overcast cool conditions and no hills for the rest of the journey, the miles tick off quickly. We start a countdown, announcing each mile marker as we pass it by. Eventually it becomes too hard to watch the markers, knowing how close we are, and still how far it seems. So we start to look for other things, like tarantulas, horses, rabbits, and cows.

With 13 miles to go, a group of horses decides to run with us. I take a photo for Michelle and Nate to let them know how excited we are about their engagement. Thirteen is their lucky number!

With only 10 miles to the border, it starts to pour rain. John decides to tough it out, while I get in my rain gear because it's cold.

Then . . .

We reach Border Patrol.

There isn't a clear place to end, so we decide to bike through the border and into Mexico. There are no cars and it's odd because we don't see any people either. When we get to the border, they ask us where we're going. We tell them we just want to take a quick loop, and then come back into the US. They must have thought we were nuts, as they let us enter Mexico and bike our loop from US soil to Mexico and back. When we bike through the US border patrol, I ask them to stamp our passports, but they laugh at us and tell us that they only do that in airports.

We take shelter from the rain under the covered porch at the US Border Patrol and take turns changing out of our wet clothes and into our casual outfits that we have worn and washed several times over the past 46 days.

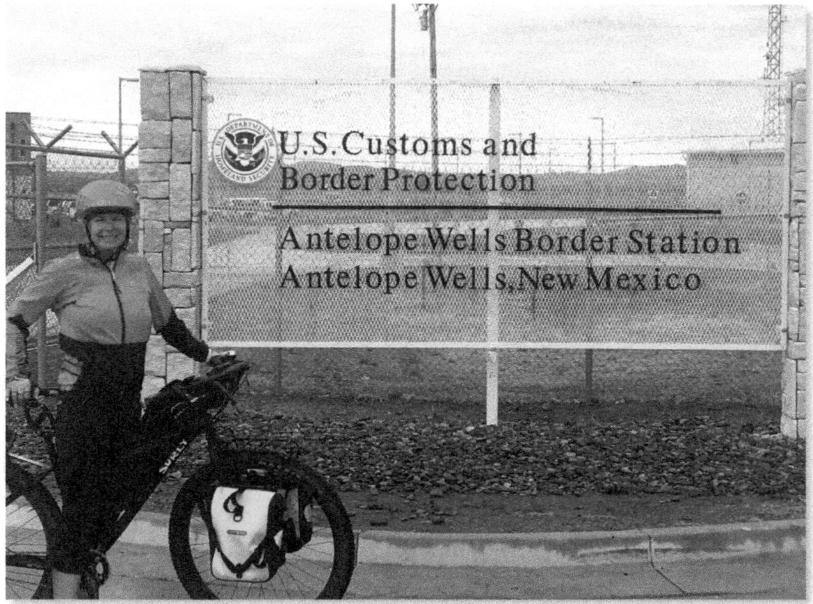

The emotion of completing the journey has left me exhausted, so I roll out my sleeping bag and take a nap. John chats with the head of the patrol and hangs out with the guy's dogs. In celebration of our accomplishment, the man buys us an ice cream sandwich and a soda. He tells us he lives on property nearby, and that because so many people just leave their dogs behind as they cross the border, he ends up adopting them—currently supporting eight dogs.

John and Tashia, John's parents, arrive at the border to pick us up. Horn honking, the rented minivan is decorated with lots of congratulatory signs. Tashia has made fresh gazpacho and brought plenty of ice-cold water and Gatorades for us. The three-hour car ride to El Paso, where we will board our flight home, absolutely flies by as we share our tales of the trail with them. Our stories trigger their own biking memories, and they tell us some of their favorites.

We talk about what it will be like to re-enter "normal" life, and what to say to people when they ask, "How was the trip?"

"They don't want to hear seven weeks' worth of stories," John's dad says. "They just want a quick recap of what it was like."

So we talk about some easy points that people would want to hear, like:

- How many days did it take you? 46
- What was your average daily distance? 60 miles
- How many flat tires? Zero
- How much weight did you lose? About 20 pounds each

Soon enough, we are entering the city of El Paso. We check in to the hotel and take a long hot shower. John is ready to shave off his beard, but that will have to wait until we get back to Denver.

It still hasn't sunk in that we have just accomplished an amazing feat. Our bodies show the evidence, though—tanned in weird places, aching muscles here and there, and the feeling of being emotionally drained. It is extra special to get picked up by John's parents. They were so excited to hear our stories—and we are grateful, once again, for the support they always show.

Ending day stats:

Start 7:30 a.m. Finish 11:45 a.m.
4 hours and 15 minutes
46.36 miles

The Journey Continues Day 1

Waking up at the hotel in El Paso feels normal. We have stayed in many hotels just like this one, and our routine kicks in. We get up, get dressed, and head to breakfast. But that's where our old normal ends.

This is our new normal. We do not have to rush through breakfast or get ready to bike for a full day. Instead, we can enjoy a relaxing breakfast with John and Tashia and then casually pack everything before heading to the airport.

Looking down from the plane, we marvel at how quickly the hilly, muddy, sunny, stormy, ragged, rocky 600-plus miles below us vanish in our wake. We know how that earth feels under our tires, though from up here it looks so small—something we could brush our hands across.

In Denver we are picked up by our daughter, Michelle, and our best friend, John Farnam. The hugs are long and powerful.

We did it.

Michelle had called me a "badass" on Facebook about halfway through the journey, and that became the nickname John used for me from then on. On particularly difficult days, he would refer to me as a badass—and today I actually feel like one. Many of the people we met on the trail only did a section of the route. Others we met decided to quit for various reasons. We stuck with it and finished it, and that feeling is starting to sink in.

The next few days are filled with more greetings from friends and family, and we slowly return to our normal lives. We want to ease into the responsibilities of everyday life, and avoid getting overwhelmed with some of the stresses that life can bring. However, as the days go on, John and I are both overcome with a strange feeling, as if the journey was actually just a dream, and that it never happened. We have to look at the photos on my phone to confirm that it was real.

The aches and pains go away. We return to the same office, the same restaurants, and order the same food—this is normal life.

So What's Next?

Upon returning home, I immediately resign from three nonprofit boards I've been on for some time. I had given this deep thought over the course of the trip, and this was the first step toward living life a little more slowly.

The next thing I need to figure out is what kind of workout I'm going to commit to after this trip. So I did what any athlete would do after such a long journey—I joined a new gym. Orange Theory. I need that high-intensity workout; I need that blood-pumping, sweat-inducing, addictive adrenaline rush that I get after a great workout. So I sign up for what I need. I do some research to see if there is a way to maintain my level of fitness (without working out for eight hours a day), but I don't find any. All of the endurance workouts and tips I find are for *building* endurance, not maintaining it. And I don't think it's realistic to train for eight hours a day . . . forever.

The first day back I take the day off and get a massage and facial. I meet with our staff at mindSpark Learning, and just enjoy visiting friends and hearing their stories about their summer. I felt like we had missed so much, but also gained so much. Michelle was now engaged and we had a wedding to plan. By Friday of the first week home we are looking at wedding dresses for the bride-to-be and enjoying the things that parents of the bride get to enjoy.

Normally after a few days in Denver we are ready to get up to our ranch. This time is different. Neither of us wants to leave the city. We don't want to leave our friends, or our family, in a great city we enjoy calling home. So we stay. Hurry is something we are trying to give up, and this really only happens once you have been unplugged for a while, or have reached a maturity in age when it's okay to slow down and do what you want to do.

After a few days off the mountain bike, I feel super eager to bike again. Just a tip—don't bike across the country if you don't enjoy biking! I love to bike, therefore getting right back on the bike was easy for me and I couldn't wait. When we reach our ranch I am overcome with emotion, as this is where it all started.

Then the big questions come: Which path do I ride? Which bike do I take? How long should my first ride be? I decide to do a short ride—two hours. I leave by myself and head straight up Route 129, which is the alternative route on the GDMBR. John is still sore and needs more time to heal, so the first few bikes in Colorado are on my own. My mountain bike (the one I use for single track) seems light as a feather. I clip my shoes into the pedals, and this alone is a huge adjustment to get used to, just like normal life.

Mentally, I decide not to turn on my computer until I feel truly ready. I think about the things I might be behind on, but it's overwhelming. So I stayed unplugged for a few more days. As I bike up to the town of Columbine, I can feel how much stronger I am. It feels like I'm floating on the bike.

It feels good to be back in the saddle again.

Most of the GDMBR was so hard it wasn't fun. I missed the fun of biking, but today, back on single track, I am having fun. Anyone who has mountain biked with me will tell you my ultimate favorite ride is Prospector Trail. Just a few miles up a dirt road to Hahns Peak, Prospector is not for sissy lalas. It is a windy, rocky, muddy, curvy slice of single-track heaven. As I make the turn to go downhill, I realize how off my timing is on single track. I'm not yet accustomed to being on a shorter bike, with different brakes, and clipped in. When I put some weight on the brakes, I nearly go head over. My back tire comes off the ground like a bucking bronco, and it takes all the power I have to force it back down. So I start taking the curves a little slower, and in the rocky sections I actually clip out and walk. Can you imagine not getting hurt at all on a trip across the country and then breaking something on your body just up the road from your home?

Our current conversations are about how to live more, how to love more, and how to enjoy what we have more. We decide what's next for us is to continue the journey—just not so dang hard! We loved the outdoors and the new routes and people we met along the way. We want to keep the journey going.

We decide to take our next trip in an RV. Coupled with a plan to take time off from work, traveling in a motorhome will be a good way to see the country and to keep things going—the journey of teamwork, of depending on each other, of finding delight in the unknown and unexpected surprises. So just 20 days after we finish, we will rent an RV and head back to one of our favorite places on the Great Divide Mountain Bike Route.

When John asks me if we will bike the Boreas Pass again, my answer is, "Heck yeah—I can't wait to do it again!"

Today marks two weeks since we have been home. There hasn't been a night we don't look at the photos and talk about the great memories. As 5:00 p.m. comes around each day, I think back to all the times on the trail I told myself, "Just two more hours—you can do it."

I am forever changed, and I hope to stay in this state of mind for as long as I can. The best bit of advice I can share with you is that if you ever have an opportunity to go on your own journey, whatever that may be—TAKE IT. Life is quick, and if you don't do it now, you might have regrets. Don't let life pass you by; grab the trail of life and live it. The adventure is waiting for you.

I hope to see you out there.

About the Authors

Carrie Morgridge is the Chief Disruptor of the Morgridge Family Foundation. Since 2008, when the Foundation was established, Carrie and her husband, John, have defined the philanthropic focus of the foundation as investing in leaders who are transforming our world through their community. She graduated summa cum laude from International Academy of Design and Technology, giving her an edge on design innovation. She is the award-winning author of *Every Gift Matters: How Your Passion Can Change the World.*

Carrie speaks nationally to education advocacy forums, at poverty alleviation conferences, and many convenings, globally, that are philanthropically focused.

Carrie imagined and founded, with John, the Student Support Foundation, a youth philanthropy club designed to cultivate high school and college philanthropists to educate and teach them the importance of giving through hands-on learning. Carrie also served an integral role in the creation of mindSpark Learning, which has provided thousands of hours of high-quality, creative, professional learning for educators from across the country. Carrie serves as chair of the board of directors of mindSpark Learning.

In 2010, Carrie Morgridge received the distinguished Frances Wisebart Jacobs Woman of the Year award from Mile High United Way. She has served on the Board of Trustees at the University of Denver, the Denver Museum of Nature and Science, Colorado Mountain College Board of Overseers, and New Jersey Center for Teaching and Learning. She has been publicly recognized for her work at National Jewish Health and Denver Academy.

Carrie is an avid outdoorsman and aggressive athlete, finishing nine ironman competitions, several marathons, Muddy Buddy, and Warrior Dash. She and John split their time between Colorado, where their two children live, and Florida.

. . .

Ross Sellers is a writer by trade and an adventurer in spirit. He earned a BA in Writing from Montana State University, with a minor in Literature. Ross has enjoyed travel throughout China and New Zealand, and volunteered extensively with Habitat for Humanity in Cambodia—though in none of these countries did he spend hours on a bike. Ross was fortunate to meet Carrie through his work with mindSpark Learning, and honored to work with her on this book.

About the Morgridge Family Foundation

The Morgridge Family Foundation is a private family foundation. The focus of the foundation is to invest in transformative gifts, thus allowing non-profits from across the United States to reach their full potential. The Foundation has taken a leadership-funding role in projects with the Denver Museum of Nature and Science, National Jewish Health, University of Central Florida, University of Denver, Mile High United Way, KIPP Schools nationwide, The Nature Conservancy, and Second Harvest Food Bank in Orlando, Florida.

100% of all proceeds from this book are given directly to Adventure Cycling Association.

www.adventurecycling.org

For more information, and pictures and videos from *The Spirit of the Trail* please visit MorgridgeFamilyFoundation.org.

CPSIA information can be obtained
at www.ICGtesting.com
Printed in the USA
BVHW02s0131180918
527384BV00017B/17/P